THE

Vintage Farmhouse Garden

29 28 27 26 25   1 2 3 4 5

ISBN: 978-0-7603-9513-4

Digital edition published in 2025
eISBN: 978-0-7603-9514-1

Library of Congress Cataloging-in-Publication Data available.

Design and Layout: Merideth Harte
Front and back cover photography: Linn Images
Photography: Candace Rhea Photography: pages 4, 25, 36, 69, 89, 95 (middle left & middle right), 114, 115, 117, 120 (top), 126 (top & bottom), 127 (middle & bottom), 138 (middle), 167
Lee Kris: page 172
Linn Images: pages 6–22, 26–29, 31–35, 38–54, 56, 58 (left), 59–61, 63, 65–68, 71 (right), 72–73, 75–88, 90–94, 95 (top left & bottom right), 96–113, 116, 118, 120 (bottom), 121–125, 126 (middle), 127 (top), 128–137, 138 (top & bottom), 139–160, 161 (bottom & top left), 162, 164, 166, 168, 171, 174–205
Oz Gurdonmaz: page 57
Rhonda Kaiser: pages 70, 71 (left), 161 (top right)
Shutterstock: pages 55, 165, 169
Steve Byland: page 170
Illustration: Jenna Lechner. jennalechner.com

Printed in China

THE

Vintage Farmhouse Garden

YOUR GUIDE TO
CREATING A VINTAGE-INSPIRED
OUTDOOR SPACE

Rhonda Kaiser
SOUTHERN HOME AND FARM

COOL
SPRINGS
PRESS

CONTENTS

The greenhouse and tool shed just beyond the blooms of the rose arch

Introduction

Hello! My name is Rhonda Kaiser, and I am the face behind Southern Home and Farm (southernhomeandfarm.com), curating my vintage farmhouse life and sharing my expertise in interior design, landscape design, and gardening, and showcasing vintage finds.

I welcome novice to expert gardeners to learn more about my vintage farmhouse life. I share scenery from my home, farm, and garden.

I love to share my knowledge, grow beautiful things, and give back to my community, while encouraging others to do the same.

After graduating from Texas A&M University, I studied interior design at the Art Institute of Houston. Working at my husband's grandmother's corner flower shop in Bishop, Texas, I found my true passion in floral design. This sparked my desire to deepen my knowledge of gardening and decorating. I became certified as a Texas Master Gardener, and my husband and I bought a 60-acre (24 ha) farm. The farm is my peaceful escape from life, the perfect setting for curating all things garden and home, as well as vintage style and design.

↑ *I enjoy caring for my raised zinnia bed, pictured here in the summer.*

I have always dreamed of writing a book, and feeling a sense of joy and pride seeing my name on the cover and having my work displayed. With all the gardening expertise I have acquired, I decided now is the perfect time.

Outdoor spaces extend your living areas, seamlessly blending comfort and nature. I've designed my home and outdoor areas with a casual, relaxed atmosphere. I hope my book will give you the tools to create your own beautiful outdoor environment filled with vintage treasures, cozy corners, and a flourishing garden.

I'm excited to share my vision, inspire you, and help make your efforts tranquil and easier. I am grateful for your time spent exploring these pages.

You can find me on Instagram @southernhomeandfarm or at SouthernHomeandFarm.com

Be sure to sign up for my Free Garden Planning and Design Guide, too. Whether you are just starting your gardening journey or tending established gardens, this guide is perfect for you.

I hope you'll stop by and let me know what speaks to you!

–Rhonda

Planned and Planted

A guide to designing and using the space you have, and turning your farmhouse vision into reality

"Where do I start?" This is what everyone asks. Starting your own garden can be intimidating, but I promise it's easier than you think! The key is to take it step by step. First evaluate your space and plan what to plant. Would your space be better for a kitchen garden, a large outdoor container garden, or perhaps an indoor vertical garden? Careful planning saves you a huge amount of effort. Stay realistic and pace yourself.

On our farm, we are blessed to have more than 60 acres (24 ha) for our gardens, greenhouse, toolshed, barn, antique silo, and farmhouse. If you lack space, do not fret! Bigger is not always better. The larger your gardens, the more work it takes. And you can garden anywhere, at an apartment, a subdivision, or on a farm! Start slowly and work towards your goal.

Maximizing Your Gardening Potential: How to Thrive in Any Space

Gardening can be a part of your life, no matter where you live. You can have a vintage farmhouse garden on a suburban lot, in an urban backyard, or even indoors using houseplants or windowsill herbs. It's about growing plants you love and combining them with vintage treasures and collectibles to create a cozy and charming feel. On the coming pages are some different options for starting your garden based on your space.

A charming view of the garden and rose arch in all its glory

If you live in an apartment, you can start in several ways. Use pots and saucers for your plants. Window planters are a great option too, if you have some sunlight. Make sure you have the right light specifications each plant needs. Herbs and vegetables do better in full sun, but many houseplants often prefer bright, indirect light. If light is an issue, there are many easy-growing, low maintenance houseplants. Options include monstera, peace lily, peperomia, philodendron, pothos, snake plant, spider plants, and ZZ plants, just to name a few. You can also use windowsills or balconies. Even in limited spaces, caring for plants is well worth the effort. Growing and nurturing plants feels fulfilling once you see your plants flourishing. Plus, the sense of accomplishment you'll feel as you watch your plants thrive is incredibly rewarding. So, invest a little time and effort, and let your plants brighten up your space!

Pro Tip

Plant watering stakes make it easy to water your plants. Whether you need to water them weekly, or while you are out of town, this trick is so handy! Self-watering stakes are easy to use, durable, and do the watering for you. They work with a simple but effective siphoning process. The stakes draw water up from any filled receptacle (such as a container or bottle) via a thin, weighted tube, then disperse it from a clay cone. Be sure to soak the clay cones for 15 minutes first. This method provides a steady, controlled release of water into the soil. The larger the water receptacle, the longer the plants will be watered. I've used plastic pitchers when away on vacation. You can buy the stakes from nurseries or online retailers.

↑ *The process of inserting and using watering stakes*

Gardening indoors can be both enjoyable and practical, especially when you find the right areas in your home and the right plants to go in them. If you would like to garden inside your home, there are many ways you can do so.

A south-facing window gives the best indoor lighting, encouraging growth. A bright west-facing window can often be too intense in the afternoon, especially during the summer, and may risk burning your plants.

I recommend beginning with small pots and saucers or an herb box of your own. Starting small makes indoor gardening manageable, gives you a quick sense of accomplishment, and helps you develop your gardening skills. There's something very rewarding about pinching fresh herbs right off a plant you have grown yourself and adding them directly to your cooking, elevating the flavor of your dishes and adding a touch of homegrown.

If there is no natural light, indoor herb gardening kits are a great alternative. These compact kits fit easily on a countertop and often include grow lights that imitate natural sunlight, giving your plants the light they need to thrive and grow. This way, you can create a vibrant mini garden in any part of your home, ensuring fresh herbs year-round and adding a touch of the outdoors wherever you place them.

↑ *Rosemary and angel vine topiaries*

AIR PURIFICATION

One of the many advantages of growing houseplants is their ability to purify the air, making it fresher and healthier to breathe. Plants do so via the process of *photosynthesis*. Plants take in the carbon dioxide we breathe out, along with water and sunlight, to create energy. During this process, plants release oxygen, which we then breathe in. This natural exchange not only freshens the air but also contributes to reducing airborne toxins. Reducing toxins significantly improves our indoor air quality, creating a cleaner and fresher environment.

VERTICAL GARDENING

If you have only a small parcel of land, there is a simple way to expand your gardening space: Think vertically! Not only does vertical gardening lead to a fruitful harvest, it can also create a visually stunning space. Bean towers, A-frames, cages, obelisks, fences, or trellises optimize your garden space beautifully. Hanging baskets and wall-mounted containers are excellent options, too.

You'll wrestle with fewer weeds when you expand your garden vertically, a major plus.

If you use bean towers or other tall structures, you'll want to grow climbing plants. Some of my favorite memories from when my daughter was growing up involve us harvesting our sugar snap peas. She always loved how the tendrils curled around the support structure. It just goes to show

Pro Tip

Create your own rustic obelisk by anchoring three sturdy branches in the ground. Secure them together at the top with wire. Then, use additional wire to attach smaller twigs, crisscrossing them along each side to complete the structure.

that gardening can be calming and enjoyable for you, while also being educational and fun for your little ones.

WIDE OPEN SPACES

If you have ample acreage, the sky's the limit! When my husband and I started using the land on our farm, I grabbed a pencil and a piece of paper to sketch out a rough idea of the space we had and wrote down measurements of the garden area. If you are feeling ambitious, use an architectural scale ruler to get exact dimensions to scale. After this, I sketched out a very rough idea of how I wanted to arrange my garden. I have always found visualizing my space really helps when planning, so why not start with putting your ideas on paper? If you want more sophistication, you can buy gardening software programs. Typically, you simply put in your perimeter dimensions and drag digital plant illustrations where you want them to go. Always plan for the mature size of a plant, as some can grow quite tall or wide. Examples of plants like these include squash, watermelons, pumpkins, and cantaloupe. Their vines always take over a space very quickly. While they are tiny at first, it is imperative you give them lots of room to flourish and grow.

↑ *An A-frame and bean tower supporting cucumbers and squash*

↑ *Here's a view of our garden, showcasing the water feature and a bench accented with cozy spring pillows for a welcoming touch.*

Pathways and Seating

After planning your garden bed layout, it is essential to consider pathways and seating. Think about the type of pathways and seating you build. Would you rather they be aesthetically pleasing or purely functional? While wider paths are best for strolling, smaller pathways will optimize planting space. Always allow at least eighteen inches (46 cm) between garden beds, just enough for a wheelbarrow to pass through. If your garden needs to be accessible to people with disabilities, ensure that the pathways fit the mobility device. For example, the American Disabilities Act suggests a minimum sixty-inch (1.5 m) turning radius for a wheelchair.

Also, consider a seating area. On especially hot days in the garden, it's nice to have a space to sit for a few minutes and have a cold glass of iced tea. You can also use this seating area on non-working days, when you can sit back with a good book and appreciate the beauty of your garden and enjoy the fruits of your labor.

TYPES OF PATHWAY MATERIALS

For any pathway or garden area, I first prepare the space thoroughly. I remove any weeds or grass to create a clean foundation. Next, I lay down weed barrier fabric and secure it with garden pins. Once that's done, I can fill the space with the material I want.

Pathways communicate formal or informal style. Think about the character of your garden and choose materials that complement that style. There's a wide variety of pathway materials to suit any project and budget. Here are a few options to consider:

Pro Tip

Use stakes as plant markers and top with finials or small pots so you don't hurt yourself while bending down.

↑ *Clay pots atop garden markers where my Itoh peonies are planted*

- **Decomposed granite.** This is what I use around my garden and in my pathways. I have found that once it compacts, it really keeps weeds down, making them easy to manage. It is cost effective and low maintenance.
- **Pavers.** Pavers are sturdy, long-lasting cut stones crafted from concrete or natural stone. With their more structured appearance, pavers are an ideal choice for formal or classic garden designs.
- **Steppingstones.** Often installed in a free-form pattern, steppingstones add a decorative element and visual interest to your pathway. Steppingstone paths give a garden a more relaxed feel.
- **Mulch.** If you are looking for a more natural, organic pathway that decomposes and is low maintenance, wood chip or shredded bark mulch is a good choice. It is also one of the most economical options. However, because it decomposes, you must replenish it every few years. Fill your pathway with at least three inches (8 cm) of mulch.
- **Brick.** Ideal for more formal gardens, brick is durable and deters weeds. Herringbone and basket weave are two traditional, popular design patterns.
- **Small stones or pebbles.** Small stones and pebbles are budget-friendly options that also offer excellent drainage, making them a practical choice for pathways.

If you're worried about your chosen pathway material spreading into your lawn, consider adding metal or stone edging. This helps contain the material and gives your space a polished, well-defined look.

Your initial focus should be to determine the layout, size, and pathways of your garden. Here's how to take those factors into account:

1. Diagram your space to plan what will fit into it.
2. Design with gentle curves rather than straight lines. Curves are more pleasing to the eye. For vegetable garden layouts, symmetry is best.
3. Optimal vegetable bed size for good yields is at least three feet by three feet (1 m by 1 m). Larger beds work, too, if you have room for them, but a four foot (1.2 m) maximum width is ideal because you can easily reach across the bed to plant or weed.
4. Locate your garden beds close to your home and an easily accessible water source. You can also install rainwater collection barrels.
5. Choose a location with at least six to eight hours of sunlight a day. Plants such as herbs and roses need full sun. Location is key!

Planning Your Space

After designing the basics of your garden space, it's time to think about the plants you want to grow. Start by finding your property's *hardiness zone*, as well as developing a *planting schedule* suited to your particular climate.

HARDINESS ZONES AND THEIR SIGNIFICANCE

Your United States Department of Agriculture (USDA) plant hardiness zone dictates which plants are best suited to your climate, saving you time, money, and frustration. You can find the map easily online. To find your hardiness zone, search the site with your ZIP code. Hardiness zones also tell you the average annual minimum winter temperature ranges of different regions of the United States. This is critical to know if you want your roses, hydrangeas, shrubs, and other perennials to survive the winter. One tricky aspect of hardiness zones is that they appear to be shifting slightly under climate change.

In your hardiness zone, the number of days between the average last spring frost date and the average first fall frost date tells you the length of your growing season. My northern friends have shorter growing seasons than in the South. This means there are fewer crops they can grow before the winter. Northern plants must mature inside of two or three months. Southern gardeners can choose plants that take longer to mature. The warmer southern climate also allows multiple growing seasons. One caveat: Intense summer heat can be tough on plants.

A view of our summer garden with our American Paint Horse, Fancy

CHOOSING THE RIGHT PLANTS

Choose your plants based on your hardiness zone. Plants are also assigned hardiness zones in online catalogs and at nurseries. Pick only the ones that thrive in your zone.

A good planting schedule tells you what to plant and when to plant it. You can find your planting schedule online by typing "planting schedule for USDA hardiness zone X" where X is your zone number. This simple search reveals *what you can plant* and *when you can plant it* according to other gardeners and experts in your location.

You can then develop a list of possible plants for your garden and narrow down the best times for growing them. For a vegetable garden, a planting schedule also helps you determine when to start seeds, transplant, and harvest.

EVALUATING YOUR SPACE

Next evaluate your space. Is it shady or sunny? Small or large? Do you have a nearby water source? Using your plant list, cross out plants that don't fit the conditions of your space. If a plant prefers to live in moist soil but your space is very dry, this plant would not be happy in your garden. Again, keep in mind mature plant

Pro Tip

If you are a novice or you're starting a new vegetable garden from scratch, use nursery transplants rather than seeds. These mature much faster than seeds and lessen the learning curve for new gardeners.

sizes when surveying your area (see Wide Open Spaces on page 14). Some plants grow very large. Make sure all plants have room to grow.

After this, decide if you want flowers or vegetables. Or both. If you want only edible crops, of course you cross off any plants that don't produce food. You will slowly cull your list to the ones perfect for you and your garden.

You'll learn more about how I planned my garden and how I lay out each of my planting beds in both the spring and the fall in chapter 2 on page 62.

Put Your Gardening Gloves On

Now it's time to dig. Soil preparation is the most crucial aspect of gardening. It boosts root development, helps plants take up more nutrients and water, and helps prevent pests and diseases. Good soil structure helps roots grow long and deep. Preparing your soil properly is the best thing you can do to give your plants a strong head-start in life.

SOIL PREPARATION

An old gardening adage tells us, "Never put a $10 plant in a $2 hole!" This means don't plant an expensive plant in a hole where you have made no effort to improve the soil. High quality soil yields a bountiful and healthier harvest. High quality soils are well draining, fertile, and moisture retentive. Poor soil has insufficient nutrients and drainage. The best way to boost soil quality is to add organic matter: any material that was originally part of a living organism. Examples include compost, shredded leaves, grass clippings, manure, wood chippings, sphagnum peat moss, and even kitchen scraps. Organic material helps retain moisture and nutrients while slowly decomposing and adding nutrients over time. If you have compacted soil, such as clay- or silt-based soil, organic matter can loosen it, making it easier for roots to penetrate. Soil conditioners, such as kelp meal or earthworm castings, are some more nutrient-rich soil amendments.

Do you have clay, sand, silt, or loam? What's the difference? Clay soil drains very slowly. Sandy soil drains quickly, has a coarse texture, and retains few nutrients. Silt soil consists of nutrient-rich, dust-like particles. It retains water better than sandy soil. Loam has a balanced mixture of sand, silt, and clay particles. It's fertile, well draining, and easily workable.

↑ *High-quality soil is a must in the garden for your plants to thrive and grow!*

So how do you determine your soil type? You can order a soil test from your county's agricultural extension office for free or for a nominal fee. Once you have determined your soil type, you can then amend it based on this information.

Pro Tip

Be sure to read the pot tags that come with most plants. They have valuable planting information and care instructions, including the plant's name as well as light, water, and spacing requirements.

FILLING MY RAISED BEDS

I prefer using raised beds whenever possible. A higher bed drains faster, so plants will develop stronger, deeper root systems. Raised beds are also easier to amend than digging in the ground. And easier on your back! First, remove grass and weeds. Place weed fabric down over the area and secure it with landscaping pins. Weed fabric hinders weed growth, and I have found it to be effective in my garden. Then put your raised bed frame down over that area.

You can buy or make a frame out of lumber. We used two inch by twelve inch (5 by 30 cm) pressure-treated lumber, which is safe for gardening. Older pressure-treated lumber may not be recommended, as the chemicals can leach into the soil. To assemble the corners, we used four inch by four inch by eight inch (10 by 10 by 20 cm) interior posts at each corner and secured them with lag screws. My garden includes two four foot by six foot (1 by 2 m) beds and four four foot by eight foot (1 by 2.4 m) beds. Make sure your bed is no wider than four feet (1.2 m) so you can reach across it.

Next, add a high-quality, raised-bed-specific soil mix. I use a homemade mixture of equal parts peat moss, coarse vermiculite, and blended compost. Then I till it thoroughly. I recommend tilling raised beds at least twice a year to keep the growing medium light and fluffy, once in the spring and again in the fall. If you do not have a mechanical tiller, you can use a garden fork or a shovel. For another way to fill raised beds, see the sidebar on *hügelkultur* on page 24.

Make sure to add organic matter to the soil each season, too. When soil is rich and fertile, your plants will be more productive and you can deter weeds, manage pests and diseases, and provide good soil aeration. It is also important to mulch your beds after planting. To do so, cover the top of the soil in a layer of mulch, such as shredded leaves or straw, to retain moisture, reduce weeds, and improve growing conditions. Not only is mulch functional, but it looks nice.

Pro Tip

For indoor seed starting, a sterile growing mix is best. If you would like to make your own, use equal parts horticultural-grade vermiculite, milled sphagnum peat moss, and perlite. Be sure to keep this medium slightly moist when sowing your seeds.

→ *These bok choy seedlings were planted indoors under grow lights in a sterile potting mix and are now ready for the garden.*

After taking into account your climate, space, and soil, you are ready to plant. Do you want to plant annuals or perennials? What's the difference?

Annuals are plants that sprout from seed, mature, and die in one growing season.

There are two types of annuals: warm season and cool season. Warm-season annuals germinate in the spring, flower, and then die come autumn. Cool-season annuals germinate in the fall, and may survive the winter, and then complete their one-year growing cycle by flowering, setting seed, and dying the following spring. Many plants grown as annuals are technically perennials. In areas with cold winters, these plants are grown as annuals because they do not survive freezing temperatures. Plants in this category include lantana, coleus, crotons, Rex begonias, and even tomatoes and peppers. Whether you grow true annuals or grow freeze-sensitive perennials as annuals, annuals are meant to adorn your garden for just one growing season. Annuals last longer in the South. One thing to keep in mind is that annuals are typically higher maintenance than perennials.

Here are some of my favorite annuals, selected for their seasonality and ideal growing conditions:

- **Top annuals for summer heat:** Celosias, crotons, sunflowers, gomphrena, lantanas, pentas, purslane, and zinnias.
- **Best shade-tolerant annuals:** Begonias, caladiums, coleus, elephant ears, and impatiens.
- **Cool-season annuals:** Dusty miller, ornamental cabbage, pansies, petunias, snapdragons, stock, sweet alyssum, Swiss chard, and violas.

Perennials are plants that live more than two years. Some perennials live only four to six years; others live for decades. Make sure the perennials you choose are winter hardy in your growing zone. I primarily focus on my vegetable and flower gardens, so many of my plants are annuals. However, if you are landscaping a large yard, it's always prettier and lower maintenance to combine annuals and perennials.

Here are some of my favorite perennials for different growing conditions:

- **Top perennials for sunny spots:** Chrysanthemums, daylilies, ornamental grasses, hardy hibiscus, iris, lamb's ear, purple coneflowers, salvias, sedums, and yarrow.
- **Best perennials for shady areas:** Columbine, ferns, four o'clocks, hellebores, hostas (my favorite variety is 'Guacamole'), spider lilies, summer phlox, and sweet violets.

THE *HÜGELKULTUR* METHOD

In German, *hügelkultur* means "hill cultivation." The *hügelkultur* method started in Germany and eastern Europe. This traditional gardening method involves creating a planting bed with layers of whole organic materials *before* adding soil on top. Farmers used it to maximize their harvests. Many gardeners still use this method today.

The basic method is to layer various organic materials and then top them with soil. It is a great way to use saved materials to efficiently fill a lot of space. From bottom to top, a *hügelkultur* bed consists of 40 percent large logs, 20 percent small branches, 25 percent plant trimmings, 10 percent compost, and 5 percent topsoil. The benefits include improved soil conditions as the materials break down, better water retention, cost-effectiveness, and environmental friendliness.

I use *hügelkultur* in my gardens to fill raised beds and large containers. Here's the process I followed when I decided to plant eight 'Eden Climber' roses around all eight columns surrounding our grain silo:

1. I started with a large container: Use containers with a diameter of more than twenty inches for the best results (smaller containers can simply be filled with soil). Begin by placing larger logs at the bottom, filling 40 percent of the container. This helps retain moisture and nutrients as the wood decomposes over time. If larger logs are unavailable, use pine nuggets or another coarse organic material.

2. Then I added smaller branches: Smaller branches made up 20 percent of the container. Gradually I added even smaller branches.

3. Next came nutrient-rich material, then a 25 percent layer of nutrient-rich plant materials such as grass clippings, leaves, and prunings.

4. Compost layer: I added a 10 percent layer of compost, which can include well-rotted manure or compost.

5. Topsoil and mulch: Finally, a 5 percent layer of high-quality topsoil, packing it until it was roughly two inches lower than the rim of the container to prevent soil spillage when watering. Compact the soil by patting it down. Top with mulch if you'd like.

↑ *I used the* Hügelkultur *method described on the facing page to plant the 'Eden' climbing rose beneath the silo post.*

Earning Your Green Thumb

The easiest way to develop a green thumb is to tend your garden and plants properly. Let's look at some of the garden maintenance tasks you'll need to practice growing the garden of your dreams.

WATERING

It is best to water in the mornings, when it's coolest, and before the heat of the day starts evaporating the water. Watering early gives the water time to soak into the soil before the heat of the sun, which can burn plant leaves. Watering early also gives your plants enough time to dry off before nighttime. Wet leaves invite diseases and pests. You can also keep your leaves dry by watering at the base instead of from above.

If you can't water in the morning, you can use soaker hoses or drip irrigation systems. These release water slowly, right to the roots, never wetting the leaves. Drip watering systems also conserve water, making them more environmentally sustainable. And they are a real advantage in a water-restricted area.

Pro Tip

When layering logs into a *hügelkultur* setup, avoid using rot-resistant woods such as black cherry, black locust, black walnut, or cedar. They do not readily decompose and can be harmful to plants. Suitable woods include alder, apple, birch, cottonwood, dry willow, maple, oak, and poplar.

NOURISHING YOUR GARDEN: FERTILIZING AND COMPOSTING

When fertilizing your crops, organic fertilizers are the best ones to use. They release their nutrients slowly and are made from natural ingredients. But you can use commercial synthetic fertilizers as well. Again, a quick Internet search can help you choose which fertilizer is best for your soil, your planting schedule, and your zone. An occasional dose of fish or kelp emulsion adds trace elements into the soil, which help your plants thrive. Usually, if you've properly prepared your soil and added lots of organic matter, you may not need any more fertilizers.

Start a compost pile if you want a natural fertilizer that comes straight from your own hands. Compost is great for your garden because it releases nutrients as it breaks down. You can make compost by layering different organic materials in a pile or bin occasionally adding small amounts of soil and water. As your compost ingredients begin to break down and sink down in the bin, add more organic material. Keep doing this, as well as occasionally turning the compost to aerate it, until it is ready. You will know your compost is ready when you can no longer recognize the original material. The compost should now be moist, dark brown, and crumbly, with a rich, earthy smell. There should be no unpleasant odors. In anywhere from three to six months, your compost is ready, and you can spread it in your garden. Mix the compost into your soil and wait for your plants to thrive.

↑ *A relaxing morning in the garden watering my raised beds*

MAKE THE MOST OF MOTHER NATURE

Have you ever noticed that plants look healthier and more vibrant after a rain shower? There's a reason for that! Rainwater contains *nitrate,* a natural form of nitrogen that plants absorb through their roots and leaves to support green growth. So, next time rain is on the way, consider moving your indoor potted plants outside to give them a healthy dose of nitrate.

USE NATIVE AND
DROUGHT-TOLERANT PLANTS

We are losing native plant populations rapidly due to urban development and herbicide use, among other causes. Gardeners are starting to learn the benefits of growing native plants, which provide habitat for wildlife and require little or no maintenance. Cultivating a small native-plant-filled habitat in your yard is very rewarding. To start one, visit wildflower meadows, trails, lakes, etc., to see what native species grow there. Or go to a specialty nursery that works with native plants in your area. The goal here is to use the kinds of native plants you find.

→ *Succulent plants, like those growing in this old wringer washer, require less water and fertilizer than many other garden plants.*

Pro Tip

During growing season, vegetables require a minimum one inch (2.5 cm) of water per week, and even more during warmer months. Timers can schedule automatic watering, saving you time and effort. When you buy hoses, make sure they're durable.

MANAGING WEEDS, PESTS, AND DISEASES

These three issues vex virtually every gardener. I find that if I do not address a problem immediately, it gets worse, and then I wind up composting countless dying plants.

WEED CONTROL

To deter weeds in pathways, first place down a layer of cardboard (sans ink, as some can be harmful to your garden) or weed-blocking fabric, then cover it with at least four inches (10 cm) of mulch. Top pathways with wood chips or decomposed granite (see Types of Pathway Materials on page 16). You can apply a pre-emergent weed control product if you're not growing food nearby, but most often hand weeding and mulching are enough to keep weeds at bay.

Be sure to mulch your growing beds, too! Organic mulches include straw, leaves, grass clippings, shredded bark, compost, and wood chips. As organic mulches decompose, they improve the soil's tilth (workability), aeration, and drainage. How much to use depends upon the type, but one to two inches (3 to 5 cm) applied around growing plants is usually enough.

PEST CONTROL

Whether you prefer organic or non-organic pest control products, there is a plethora to choose from. Use what works best for you. I have found a combination works best in my garden. I like to keep things simple and use three-in-one products that combine a fertilizer (essential nutrients for plants), a fungicide (controls fungi that harm plants, such as rusts, mildews, blights, and molds), and a miticide (pest control for mites). Ask your local garden center to help select the most appropriate controls for your garden based on your garden's issues. Their staffs are often very knowledgeable.

DISEASES

As discussed on page 25, watering in the morning to keep foliage dry is one of the best ways to prevent and manage diseases. Space plants properly to provide good air flow and clean up and remove any diseased leaves to prevent any disease from spreading. For tougher issues, choose a fungicide product and use according to the label instructions.

Gardening Gems and Extra Tips

Here are some additional pieces of advice to help you plan and grow a successful garden. They come from my own experiences and are important for bringing it all together.

SUCCESSION PLANTING

Succession planting involves planting the same crop several times in one season. You plant each crop as the previous crop is beginning to mature. When the original planting is going by, the new planting starts to mature. Succession planting is especially beneficial if you live in a climate with a particularly long growing season.

Succession planting works especially well with carrots. You can keep the carrots coming for many months by planting seeds every three to four weeks. While you are harvesting the first batch of carrots, the next batch of carrots is coming in.

I suggest seeding your crops at intervals of seven to twenty-one days, depending on the maturing time needed for each crop. You can research maturation time by looking at seed packets or going online.

TIPS FOR HANDLING LARGER GARDEN PESTS

While deer don't usually bother us, if they're eating your dinner, sink metal hoops in the center of your garden beds to keep them away. Smaller critters like rabbits chomp away in our gardens. We try to deter them with a low, decorative fence. If birds come to your garden, you can wrap bird netting around the garden beds and over the plants. Pin the netting into the ground. We also have curious horses, so we built a split-rail cedar fence around our antique roses to keep the roses from becoming horse feed.

Small plants and seedlings are most at risk. I protect them with chicken wire cloches.

→ *Chicken wire cloches safeguard new transplants.*

VOLUNTEER PLANTS

There are also a lot of great resources online—including worksheets and templates—to help you plan out a succession planting schedule.

Volunteer plants are those that come up in the garden all on their own. These plants typically grow from seeds dropped by flowers, birds, various animals, or even the wind. Removing crowded volunteer plants helps keep your garden healthy. However, I rarely discard them! I always think of them as "bonus plants." I simply move them to a more appropriate area. If a volunteer is small enough, I will plant it in a pot. Once it gets larger, I transplant it to the garden. One of my favorite tomato varieties came from a volunteer plant, and those tomatoes are so sweet and juicy! Unfortunately, it's impossible to trace that variety back to the original plant, but I feel fortunate to have it return year after year as a volunteer!

If you are aiming to reduce the number of volunteer plants sprouting up in your garden, a few proactive steps can help manage their spread. First, consider deadheading your plants before their flowers have a chance to set seeds. By regularly removing spent blooms, you prevent them from producing seeds that could scatter throughout your garden, leading to an abundance of unwanted growth. Additionally, applying a thick layer of mulch across your garden beds can make a significant difference. Mulch not only suppresses weed growth by blocking sunlight from reaching the soil but also helps to discourage seeds from germinating in the first place.

Pro Tip

Never compost diseased plants! They can reinfect your garden! Most home compost piles don't reach a temperature high enough to kill diseases.

MATURE PLANTS AND SUNLIGHT

As I mentioned, when you plant, always consider each plant's mature size. One of the best tips is to organize plants according to their mature size. Place shorter and trailing plants in the front of the bed, medium-sized, fuller plants in the middle, and taller plants in the back. Because the sun travels across the sky, the "back" of your vegetable garden should be on its north side, and it should be filled with tall-growing crops, such as okra, staked tomatoes, pole beans, and sweet corn. These crops work best on the north side of the garden so they will not shade or interfere with the growth of lower-growing crops. Low growers include radishes, leaf lettuces, onions, and bush beans. If you layer plants this way, every plant gets ample sunlight, and you can easily see every plant. This technique is important when container planting, too.

CROP ROTATION

Never repeat your crops from season to season. Plant a different crop every season in each area. This technique is called *crop rotation*, which keeps the soil from being depleted of nutrients. Crop rotation also boosts yields and keeps soil erosion, disease, and pests to a minimum. Crop rotation is so beneficial that it is required in commercial organic crop production! So be sure to rotate vegetable crops in your garden.

Pro Tip

Use mirrors or glass to reflect light in shady areas. Keep overhead branches pruned and to a minimum. If your vegetables don't get full or nearly full sun, try growing leafy, more shade-tolerant crops such as leaf lettuce, mustard greens, kale, and parsley.

SUNFLOWER FUN

Consider training sunflowers up a three-sided trellis for a unique and playful garden tepee. Start by planting 'Mammoth' sunflower seeds in a circle, leaving a small gap for an entrance. As the sunflowers grow, gently tie or stake them together at the top to create a natural, whimsical playhouse tepee made entirely of towering sunflower stalks. This is a delightful way to engage children in gardening and spark their imaginations. I created one for my daughter when she was a toddler, and she absolutely loved it, just as any child would!

Creating an Accessible Garden

Accessible gardening means designing your garden so individuals with disabilities or limited mobility can easily enter and enjoy. Every individual, regardless of ability, can take pride in watching plants grow from seed to vegetable. In an accessible garden, people with disabilities can fully experience the beauty of the garden, as well as its many other benefits.

CURATING AN ACCESSIBLE SPACE

A key to designing an accessible space for people with disabilities is to consider the needs of each disability. Below are some starting points:

Seated gardening. Gardeners who cannot stand for long periods of time appreciate seats and benches. Benches can be ergonomically designed to fit any height or width. Raised beds at wheelchair height are helpful for individuals with wheelchairs or mobility devices.

Pathways should be firm, smooth, and level. Paths need to be a minimum of five feet (1.5 m) wide so wheelchairs can turn around. Consider including solar-powered lighting along your pathways too, for safety.

↑ *Raised beds provide an ideal gardening option for individuals with disabilities.*

ADAPTIVE GARDENING TECHNIQUES FOR GARDENERS WITH DISABILITIES

Thanks to technology, accessible gardening is fully possible. It is a great way to enrich one's lifestyle, no matter the age, stage in life, or disability. Gardening is therapeutic and provides enrichment and fulfillment. While you are designing your accessible garden, keep in mind that different disabilities require different accommodations. Below are some examples of gardening accommodations for a few different disabilities:

For visual impairments, tactile markers such as textured pavement help people find their way. The visually impaired can enjoy different leaf textures and the fragrances of lavender, thyme, basil, and lemon balm.

For limited mobility, vertical gardening makes plants more reachable. You can adjust the heights of trellises, hanging baskets, and wall-mounted planters. Climbing plants, sugar snap peas, tomatoes, beans, etc., make harvesting easier.

People with intellectual disabilities can engage with interactive features. Wind chimes or bird feeders add auditory and visual interest, making the garden a more dynamic space. Plants with soft, soothing textures offer a positive sensory experience for individuals with sensory sensitivities.

For arthritis, easy-grip tools and braces help protect wrist movement against impact and vibration. These tools stabilize the hand and wrist in their natural positions to ensure comfortable gardening. Attachable extension poles easily extend your reach. Some examples of these tools include the Easi-Grip Garden Cultivator®, the Tractor Scoot®, and any stabilizing wrist wrap.

FIVE TIPS FOR GARDENING WITH INDIVIDUALS WITH ALZHEIMER'S OR DEMENTIA

1. Safety first: Remove any gardening tools or hazards along the pathways. Also, ensure all tables and seating options are sturdy and durable.
2. Design a layout: When laying out your garden, consider creating a large loop. This ensures that all pathways lead back to your house and no one is likely to get lost.
3. Provide a peaceful environment: Your loved ones will appreciate a peaceful environment, and so will their caregivers. To create calm, add such things as wind chimes and water features.
4. Schedule gardening: Make gardening part of your loved one's daily routine, to make the garden areas familiar.
5. Keep it simple: Watering, harvesting crops, or weeding are simple, enjoyable tasks your loved ones can join in with. You can also invite your loved ones to choose which plants to grow.

Summing Things Up

Here's a quick tip list for getting started that highlights all the information in this chapter:

- Learn your hardiness zone and planting schedule for your specific microclimate.

- Cultivate your garden near your home, with at least six to eight hours of sunlight and an accessible water source.

- The key to successful gardening is soil preparation! Preparing your soil is the best thing you can do for a bountiful garden. Garden soil needs to be well drained, fertile, and moisture retentive. How do you achieve this? By adding organic matter. This can include compost, manure, peat moss, or soil conditioners.

- Water the garden every week with at least one inch (2.5 cm) of water and water more during the summer.

- Fertilizers, organic or synthetic, really get your garden growing.

- Give your plants an occasional dose of fish emulsion, which adds trace elements to the soil that help plants thrive.

- Stay on top of pests with control when necessary. Visit your local garden center to help identify and select the most appropriate controls for your garden. You can buy many organic and commercial products online.

- Keep weeds at bay in a new garden by first removing all the grass, then placing down weed fabric *before* filling the beds with soil. Add a few inches of mulch for moisture retention and more weed deterrence.

- My most important and valuable piece of advice is to enjoy the gardening process and have fun!

CREATE YOUR VISION GALLERY

Use inspiration from my garden to design and plant a garden of your own.

↑ *Lavender is a perfect selection for a fragrant and sensory garden.*

↑ *A detailed view of our garden bench adorned with hand-painted pillows, and a watering can filled with herbs, sitting atop a vintage whiskey barrel used as a small coffee table*

→ *An outside view of our greenhouse*

← *A-frame trellis with vegetable beds and rose arch*

→ *A simple wooden raised garden bed with lavender, petunias, and herbs*

Outdoor Oasis

Transforming a functional garden space into a sanctuary

After planning your garden, you can transform it into your own personal outdoor oasis! For us, this meant expansion. Our entire garden space (including the outside perimeter of roughly thirty antique roses) now measures roughly forty feet by sixty feet (12 by 18 m). This space has multiple raised beds, two four foot by six foot and four four foot by eight (1.2 by 1.8 and 1.2 by 2.4 m). These sizes are quite ambitious. So, I recommend that beginning gardeners *start small and have patience!* You can always expand later.

We expanded our garden one piece at a time, adding granite pathways, vintage double-loop ornamental wire fencing, antique gates, rose arches, container gardens, and, eventually, bistro lighting. A cedar bench with a gorgeous vintage twin-sized metal headboard is one of my favorite features. Next to it stands a repurposed whiskey barrel we use as a coffee table (for our family, really the "iced tea table"). I love to sit in this space after a long day of gardening. It's the perfect spot to soak in the fruits of my labor. All these pieces really made the garden our own, transforming it from just a typical garden to an outstanding space where we hold gatherings with family and friends.

In this chapter, we're going to explore some ways you too can take your garden to the next level and create your own outdoor oasis, no matter what size space you're working with.

Cultivating Creative Container Gardens

One simple way to personalize your garden is using container plantings. Container gardening dates to ancient Egypt. But in the late 1700s, Spanish colonists were thought to bring container gardening to New Orleans' French Quarter courtyards. Being from the South, I always enjoyed strolling through those beautiful and inspiring courtyards. My visits inspired me to start using container gardens in my space, too.

Container gardening can jazz up a garden in several ways. It adds color and texture to otherwise simply green areas. It enlivens transitional areas. And it creates interest and perspective in otherwise ordinary areas.

I fill my containers with a mix of annuals and perennials to give a pop of color to bare areas of the garden. Flowers give you a chance to brighten the garden with bold colors in creative and stylish ways.

CONTAINER GARDENING MADE EASY

Begin with a clean container with drainage holes. Put a few stones or pot shards loosely over the holes to keep the soil from escaping along with excess water. Buy high-quality potting soil; it yields much healthier plants. Fill the container with the potting soil, leaving a few inches of space at the top to prevent soil from spilling over during watering.

Now you are ready to plant!

Start with the tallest plants. Place these at the back or center of the container, depending on your vantage point. Next, arrange the fuller, shorter plants in front of or around the tall ones. Finally, add low and trailing plants along the outer edges. As a former florist, I aim for symmetry. What I place on one side, I mirror on the other. Always position the most attractive side of the plant facing the front!

RUSTIC CHARM

Looking to add a touch of rustic charm to your garden? Consider a large wicker basket as a planter. Start by spraying the basket, inside and out, with a clear sealant to extend its lifespan. Next, line it with a contractor bag (a heavy-duty plastic bag with a large capacity), and poke small holes in the bottom for drainage. Then fill it with soil.

↑ *A vintage general post office cart filled with Kimberly Queen ferns*

UNIQUE HAND-THROWN POTS

I always seek out vintage or one-of-a-kind artisan pieces whenever I can (you'll hear much more about this in the coming chapters). When I couldn't find the exact handmade garden pottery I envisioned to bring a unique feel to my garden and greenhouse, I asked my favorite potter to create my own version! Each pot is handcrafted and unique. To my surprise, I discovered I had purchased a pot from his studio over twenty years ago!

I'm drawn to the classic, clean look of natural white terracotta, a neutral that lets the plants take center stage. I requested some white terracotta pots with scalloped edges and others with a coggled edge, all proudly bearing the *Southern Home and Farm* logo. You can find these pots on my website, southernhomeandfarm.com.

↑ *Handcrafted ceramic pots for Southern Home and Farm*

Pro Tip

To ensure your smaller potted plants and hanging baskets grow evenly, rotate their containers at least once a month. Then all sides of the plant receive an equal amount of sunlight, resulting in more even growth. The plant also looks healthier and more attractive from every angle.

Must-Have Vegetables for Your Garden

Vegetables form the heart and foundation of any productive garden, yielding a wealth of fresh food. Whether you're cooking, preserving, drying, or collecting seeds for future planting, vegetables offer endless culinary possibilities. The variety of vegetables available today is endless, each with its own unique flavor, texture, and use, allowing you to experiment with new dishes or create seasonal staples that can be enjoyed year-round.

I grow a few essential vegetables that consistently thrive and yield large harvests, even in the warmer climate. These staples have become tried-and-true favorites, providing tasty ingredients for my meals and valuable seeds for next season. With the right choices and a bit of care, vegetables can transform your garden into a rich source of fresh, homegrown produce for your kitchen and lifestyle.

You might find some of my favorites work well in your garden, too.

Pro Tip

To harvest your seeds, cover seed heads with cheesecloth before they brown. Let the pods dry, then cut the stems evenly and hang them in bundles upside down. The seeds will drop into the cheesecloth, making it easy to collect, bag, and label them for next season. Never store seeds in plastic until they are completely dry because they might mold or rot. Envelopes are also good for storage, and you can buy small seed storage envelopes online or at a garden center.

WARM-WEATHER VEGETABLES FOR YOUR GARDEN

ASPARAGUS

Asparagus requires a significant time investment but is definitely worth the wait! After planting, you'll need to wait two years to harvest. Then, in early spring, harvest new spears with an asparagus knife or a very sharp kitchen knife, just below the soil line. After roughly six weeks, stop harvesting and allow the spears to grow into fern-like foliage. Leave the foliage alone until the first freeze nips it and turns it brown. Only then should you prune the ferns. In my southern climate, I typically wait until late winter/early spring to cut them back. Delaying the pruning process protects the crown and root structures that support next year's growth.

CUCUMBERS

Cucumbers are one of my favorite vegetables. There is nothing better than a cucumber and tomato salad on a warm summer day! Harvest the fruits before they become too large and bitter. Water and feed these fast-growing vines regularly to ensure they keep growing and producing in your garden. Be sure to provide trellising for this climber. If you find fruits are not developing, try hand pollinating. Cucumbers have both male and female flowers. You can hand pollinate by moving pollen from the male flowers to the female flowers using a paint brush to ensure fruit formation if pollinators are slow to do the job for you.

PEPPERS

Peppers come in a plethora of varieties. My peppers include banana, cayenne, chili pequin, green bell, jalapeno, orange bell, red bell, and serrano. You can pick some varieties when immature. Leaving most on the plant leads them to change colors and fully ripen. Did you know that a red bell pepper is simply a green bell pepper left to mature on the plant? Although peppers can be picked at any stage in the growth process, their taste differs if left to ripen. Experiment with your peppers and try harvesting at all stages to determine your preferred harvest time frame. Typically, the more ripened a pepper, the hotter it tastes. (See page 200 for my Authentic Jalapeño Salsa recipe).

TOMATOES

While we often think of tomatoes as vegetables, they are technically fruit. Botanically, tomatoes contain seeds, classifying them as fruit. However, in a unique 1893 U.S. Supreme Court case regarding import taxes applied to vegetables but not fruit, the tomato was legally reclassified as a vegetable. The court ruled the botanical origins of the tomato a "fruit of the vine." No matter how you classify them, tomatoes remain my favorite garden producers! I highly recommend experimenting with as many varieties as possible. Some of my top picks include 'Big Beef', 'Celebrity', 'Cherokee Purple', 'Indigo Cherry', 'Juliet', 'Roma', and my all-time favorite, 'Super Sweet 100' cherry tomatoes.

Tomato varieties are classified into *determinate* and *indeterminate*. The main differences are how they look, grow, and produce fruit.

- **Determinate** tomato plants grow to a certain size, then stop producing. Determinate tomato plants are more compact and bushier, bearing fruit earlier in the season. While some gardeners believe they may be less flavorful, they are still very popular. Varieties include 'Celebration', 'Easy Slice', 'Heatmaster', 'Paisano', 'Roma', 'San Marzano', and 'Tasmanian Chocolate', just to name a few.
- **Indeterminate** tomato plants, on the other hand, grow large and vine-like, continuing to flower and produce fruit throughout the growing season until the first frost. This is a great option for gardeners who have more space. Varieties include 'Beefsteak', 'Better Boy', 'Big Beef', 'Brandywine', 'Cherokee Purple', 'Early Girl', 'Homestead', 'Indigo Cherry', 'Juliet', and 'Super Sweet 100'.

Both types require deep watering, preferably at the base of the plant, to help prevent diseases such as blossom end rot, powdery mildew, and tomato blight. Also, make sure you have enough space for indeterminate varieties, since they grow much taller and wider than determinate ones. Ensure your tomatoes receive the most direct sun as possible, to produce the highest yield.

In my studies as a Texas Master Gardener, I learned an interesting way to plant tomatoes. Rather than digging a deep hole and planting your tomatoes vertically, try the method outlined on the next page instead.

HOW TO PLANT TOMATOES USING THE TRENCH METHOD

1. Dig a trench at least six inches (15 cm) deep.

2. Remove all leaves and suckers from the lower two-thirds of the stem.

3. Lay the tomato plant sideways in the trench, leaving only the top portion exposed.

4. Gently cover the plant with soil and water thoroughly

5. Even though the plant is sideways, it will naturally grow upright.

6. Install tomato cages or stakes now, as the plants grow quickly,
   making staking harder later.

Why use this method to plant tomatoes? The answer is simple: Roots develop along the entire length of the stem of the plant, not just from the base. More roots take up more nutrients and water, resulting in a stronger plant. A stronger plant leads to increased yields and more disease-resistant growth.

SUGAR SNAP PEAS

Every year I look forward to seeing the first pod of the season. These sweet and tasty peas with edible pods are a favorite in our garden. Sugar snap peas are vigorous climbers, so support them with trellises, wire paneling, netting, or metal fencing. This gives the tendrils something easy to grab on to. Be sure to harvest the plants before the weather becomes too warm, as the plants are quick to falter thereafter. Don't leave the pods on the vine too long; they will lose their sweet flavor.

SWEET POTATOES

Sweet potatoes thrive in hot weather. They are planted from cuttings known as slips. *Slips* are the green shoots with leaves and stems that sprout from a mature sweet potato. You can buy slips from mail-order nurseries or specialty garden centers. Sweet potatoes grow best in raised beds or rows in the ground where there is full sun and well-drained soil. They are typically ready for harvest in 90 to 110 days. (See page 201 for my Old-Fashioned Sweet Potato Pie recipe.)

COOL-WEATHER VEGETABLES FOR YOUR GARDEN

BROCCOLI

A favorite cold weather staple, broccoli should be planted in early spring, or about twelve weeks before your first freeze date for a fall crop. This cool weather plant prefers at least eight hours of full sun. Be sure to harvest before the head bolts into small yellow flowers, as it will taste bitter if it does. Harvest with a sharp tool when the broccoli heads are at least six to eight inches (15 to 20 cm) in diameter. Smaller edible side shoots develop where the cut was made. After harvesting large heads, leave the plants in place so these smaller heads can grow. My preferred varieties include 'Galaxy', 'Green Comet', and 'Packman'.

CABBAGE

Plant cabbage seeds at least twelve inches apart and in late winter or early spring. Also, water well and never let them dry out. Harvest cabbage when the head is firm to the touch and roughly the size of a grapefruit. Be sure to harvest before it splits, which can send up flower stalks. Be aware of cabbage looper caterpillars and address them as soon as they are spotted. Treat with *Bacillus thuringiensis* (Bt) at first sight. Favored cabbage varieties include 'Early Jersey Wakefield', 'Ruby Ball' (red), and 'Savoy King'.

CAULIFLOWER

Cauliflower is another cool-season crop that can tolerate frosts but not hard freezes. Plant fifteen to eighteen inches (38 to 46 cm) apart in rich, well-drained soil. If you want to keep the heads white, you can try blanching. *Blanching* means covering the head to protect it from sunlight and keep it pure white. When you notice a small head begin to form in the middle of the plant, gather the larger outer leaves and tie them together around the head with garden twine. When ready to harvest, your cauliflower will be pure white. Like broccoli, harvest heads when they are six to eight inches (15 to 20 cm) in diameter.

COLLARD GREENS

For as long as I can remember, we have cooked our collards "southern style," with onion, garlic, bacon, salt and pepper, broth, and a pinch of apple cider vinegar and sugar. I look forward to it every winter! Collard greens are highly nutritious vegetables and are filled with vitamins and minerals, not to mention being low-glycemic. Be sure to fertilize the plants with a high-nitrogen fertilizer monthly for a high yield. Harvest collards starting with the lower leaves first, at the base of the plant. Collards are cold tolerant, so winter freezes enhance their flavor. (See page 202 for Southern-Style Collard Greens recipe.)

LETTUCE

So many varieties, so little time! I enjoy planting 'Buttercrunch', 'Green Ice', 'Red Sails' (beautiful color!), romaine, salad bibb, and salad bowl. Give your lettuce full sun as any amount of shade decreases yield, except in high summer when a little shade is welcome. When harvesting, be sure to harvest lower leaves first, allowing new leaves to grow from the plant's center. Watch out for aphids! They target new growth. Either wash them away with a strong burst of water from the garden hose, or spray with neem oil or insecticidal soap.

SWISS CHARD

Swiss chard is easy to grow and highly nutritious. It adds vibrant color to the garden, especially during winter when color may be sparse. It thrives in cool temperatures. Plant Swiss chard in well-drained soil with at least eight hours of sunlight. If starting the plants from seed, soak them overnight to improve and boost germination rates. Swiss chard is a high nitrogen feeder and is typically ready to harvest in about forty days. 'Bright Lights' is a reliable variety tested in my garden.

↑ *'Buttercrunch'*

↑ *'Red Sails'*

→ *Swiss chard*

A winter glimpse of our Texas garden

Herbs are a must-have in any garden, offering lush, fragrant, and flavorful foliage. I love gently brushing my hands over their leaves, as their essential oils coat my skin. Their scents are both soothing and delightful! Whether for cooking, drying, or simply for their beauty, herbs are an invaluable addition to any garden.

Here are a few growing requirements that apply to most herbs:

- Plant in full sun.
- Use well-drained soil enriched with organic matter.
- Keep them well watered; a lack of water can reduce productivity.
- Fertilize regularly for optimal growth.
- Mulch your herb beds.
- Harvest herbs at their peak to use fresh or dried.
- If you want to eat or cook your herbs, prevent them from flowering by pinching off the blooms; if allowed to flower, the leaves may become bitter.

Let's review some of my favorite herbs. I grow them in my garden beds and in containers, where they serve as companion plants or spill beautifully over the sides of their pots.

↑ *Basil*

MY FAVORITE EASY-GROWING HERBS

Basil. One of my top picks! This warm-weather annual is known for its rich flavor. Harvest the leaves before the plant flowers to prevent bitterness. Regular harvesting promotes new growth. It's sensitive to cold, so wait until after the last frost to plant.

Chives. These slender, clumping onion relatives make a great border for beds or containers. Finely chopped chives are perfect for sprinkling over salads, potatoes, or omelets.

Dill. This herb thrives in cool weather and can grow quite tall. It bolts (goes to flower) in hot temperatures, so be sure to preserve it for pickling before your cucumbers mature. I plant extra to feed swallowtail butterfly caterpillars as it is one of their favorite host plants!

↑ *Chives*

↑ *Dill*

Fennel. Harvest the stems before the plant flowers. It's drought-resistant, and all parts of the plant are usable. As with dill, I plant extra for the swallowtail butterfly caterpillars.

Garlic Chives. Garlic chive leaves are flatter than those of traditional chives and lack the hollow structure. Traditional chives have a stronger onion flavor, while garlic chives offer a milder, garlicky taste. They are drought tolerant. I allow the seed heads to remain for self-sowing in the next season.

Lavender. This herb needs well-drained soil and minimal watering, as it prefers drier conditions. Popular varieties include English, French, Spanish, and woolly lavender.

Lemon Balm. One of the easiest herbs to grow. Its fragrant, lemon-scented leaves are great in salads, soups, and stews. I love adding the leaves to freshly brewed tea.

↑ *Lemon balm*

Mint. A water-loving and easy-to-grow herb—it's almost too easy! Mint can quickly take over a garden, so it's best to plant it in pots sunk into the ground to limit its spread. It's great for both sweet and savory dishes.

Oregano. This hardy ground cover comes in many varieties. It's best harvested before flowering and needs full sun for the strongest flavor.

Parsley. I always grow Italian flat leaf and curly. Both are beautiful and have distinct flavors. Parsley is another favorite of swallowtail butterfly caterpillars, so avoid pesticides to protect them.

Rosemary. A perennial favorite of mine, rosemary comes in various types, from trailing to upright. It loves full sun and prefers a drier soil. Its delightful fragrance adds so much charm to any garden.

Thyme. I enjoy growing several varieties of thyme, including English, French, golden, lemon, and variegated types. Thyme prefers full sun and well-drained soil. Be sure to harvest before the plants come into bloom.

↑ *Italian flat-leaf parsley*

↑ *Oregano*

→ *Rosemary*

BLACKBERRIES

These bramble fruits are very easy to grow. Blackberries grow in a variety of soils but prefer slightly acidic soil. They thrive in highly organic, moist soils with good drainage. Water frequently, especially younger plants. I prefer thornless varieties for ease of harvest but note fruit production is typically higher with thorny varieties. In general, it is best to plant blackberries in the fall and at least three feet (9 m) apart. Here are a few popular thornless varieties to try:

- 'Apache' produces large, sweet berries later in the season.
- 'Natchez' produces the largest berries that ripen early.
- 'Navajo' bears small fruits but prolifically.

Pro Tip

Blackberries will not continue to ripen off the plant, so be sure to harvest your berries at the peak of ripeness.

BLUEBERRIES

These fruiting shrubs require very acidic soil. My soil is heavy with clay and almost impossible to amend sufficiently, so I grow my blueberries in containers. You'll want to know your specific soil type for prolific growth and fruiting. Blueberries thrive best in soils enriched with composted organic matter. They are not very drought tolerant due to their shallow, fibrous root system, so be sure to irrigate your blueberry bushes with at least one to two inches (2.5 to 5 cm) of water per week. Blueberries also require *cross pollination*. Plant at least two different blueberry varieties to ensure adequate cross pollination (see sidebar below) and mulch lightly with organic material.

Try these two blueberries that are popular cross-pollinator varieties if you live in a southern growing zone like mine:

- 'Brightwell' produces medium-sized berries through the beginning of summer.
- 'Tifblue' bears smaller fruit but later in the season.

CROSS POLLINATION

Did you know that some fruit-bearing plants need pollen from a second variety to produce fruit? This is called *cross pollination*. Many fruiting plants cannot self-pollinate and rely on cross pollination to bear fruit. Examples include apple, pear, and pecan trees, among others. Cross pollination can also benefit plants by boosting fruit production and promoting earlier ripening.

RASPBERRIES

These bramble fruits prefer well drained, nutrient-rich soil in a sunny location. Keeping them well watered is essential for proper growth. Bramble fruits can get very heavy, so be sure to provide trellised support. Prune annually in late winter.

The below varieties are resistant to common diseases that affect raspberries, including root rot and blight:

- 'Dorman Red' is a trailing variety that bears large fruits, and the plants are drought- and disease-resistant. A vigorous producer, perfect for cooking, preserving, or freezing.
- 'Heritage' is a large, juicy red raspberry that is great for fresh eating or baking into treats like pies or jams.

Turn to page 199 for Linzer Cookies filled with Homemade Raspberry Jam.

STRAWBERRIES

These perennial fruits grow best in loose, well-drained soil. My soil is full of clay, so I grow strawberries in a raised bed or container in my garden. In warm climates, plant strawberries in the fall and be sure to mulch. Cold-climate gardeners should plant in the spring. I mulch my strawberries with hay as we have it readily available for our horses, but you can also use compost or straw. To protect your strawberries from pesky critters, use chicken wire garden cloches or bird netting for added protection. Your soil type determines whether in-ground or container growing will work best. Contact your local agricultural extension agency or a specialty nursery to determine the best varieties for your region.

The below varieties have been high producers in my warm-climate garden:

- 'Chandler' bears high-quality fruits with a high yield early to mid-season. Ideal for desserts and freezing.
- 'Sequoia' produces large, dark red fruits with a tasty flavor. They continue to produce fruit for many months during the growing season and are best consumed fresh.

↑ *The perfect strawberry captured in the garden*

↑ Fig tree in the orchard

FRUIT TREES ON THE FARM

Fruit trees require more maintenance, but you can enjoy their bounty for years to come. Here are a few of my favorites we have planted on the farm, along with their named varieties:

FIG ('CELESTE')

Either eaten fresh or dried, this fruit, including the skin, is rich in flavor. These easy-growing, heavy-producing trees prefer fertile, well-drained soil, though they can adapt to most soil conditions. Don't let the roots of your fig trees sit in water more than twenty-four hours. This can stunt growth and eventually kill the tree. An interesting fact: Figs are unique in that their edible fruits are stem tissue, not mature ovary tissue as with most other fruits.

The variety we have on the farm is named 'Celeste', but there are many different varieties available to home gardeners, including a few hardier selections if you live in a colder climate.

CITRUS

Here's a sampling of the citrus varieties we have growing at the farm:

- **Meyer Lemon:** While technically not a true lemon, Meyer lemons are used as a substitute and are far less acidic than true lemons. Meyer lemons are not hardy in cold climates and will only grow outdoors in tropical areas, but they can be just as productive in containers. They are nearly thornless and more cold tolerant than true lemons.

- **Lime (Mexican):** Mexican lime is also called the Key lime or West Indian lime. You can grow the Mexican lime from seed, unlike most grafted lime varieties. Key limes are compact in size and produce fruit many months out of the year. Like all citrus plants, Mexican limes need protection from the cold. To protect your lime tree during the colder months, apply a thick layer of mulch around the base in the fall. When frost is predicted, use frost blankets and heat lamps to safeguard the plant during freezing temperatures.
- **Kumquat ('Meiwa'):** Kumquats fruit much of the year and are prized on the farm. These small, edible fruits are sweet and tasty, skin and all! They can be used in cooking and preserving marmalades as well. Water well just as the soil dries out and fertilize with a high-quality, time-release fertilizer. Learn from my lesson here—although they are hardy, if it freezes in your area, be sure to protect them by using frost cloths or blankets, mulch, or heat lamps. Better yet, move your tree to a protected location.
- **Mandarins (Satsuma):** Mandarins are easy to peel and have a slightly tart, delicious taste. They are hardier than most citrus but still be aware of the occasional freeze and protect as mentioned above.

Note: Citrus trees require more maintenance than most trees and require diligent pest control to thrive. Use neem oil in late winter, before spring buds flush, to manage any overwintering eggs or larvae on the trees. Neem oil can also be used during the growing season to deter pest infestations.

↑ *Peaches on a tree*

PEACH ('FLORIDA PRINCE')

Choosing the right variety of peach is crucial to fruit production. Most peach trees require high *chill hours*—the number of hours the tree is exposed to cold temperatures during its dormant phase. We are in southeast Texas, where the number of chill hours often does not meet these requirements. However, there are some varieties that require lower chill hours than others. 'Florida Prince' is my preferred choice for my low-chill region.

PEAR ('KIEFFER')

Kieffer pears are oriental hybrids commonly grown for canning, baking, and preserving. Their coarse texture makes them difficult to eat fresh off the tree, so we primarily use them to make homemade pear jam.

PERSIMMON ('FUYU')

If persimmons are not grafted, they can be quite sour, so use them primarily for canning or jams. If grafted with another variety, they can produce sweet fruits. So, what is the difference between *grafted* and *ungrafted*?

- **Grafted:** Grafting involves grafting a piece of vegetative wood from another plant onto a host rootstock. Grafting enhances fruit quality and increases disease and pest resistance. Grafted plants and trees can typically bear fruit earlier than non-grafted ones. The downsides of grafting are that trees can be smaller, more costly and may not live as long as seed-grown trees.
- **Ungrafted:** Ungrafted plants and trees are grown from seedlings. Ungrafted trees have better resistance to local climate conditions, are more economical, and may be less likely to suffer from pest and disease issues.

↑ *Pear tree in the orchard*

POMEGRANATE ('WONDERFUL')

Pomegranates are self-pollinating and produce delicious fruit in late summer to early fall. Their beautiful orange-red blossoms emerge from spring through early summer. Pomegranates require little pruning, pest or disease treatments, or fertilizing, making them an extremely easy tree to grow. Popular in the Deep South, these sweet, delicious fruits are a staple in any southern garden. In my region of Texas, they can be susceptible to sun scald from intense summer heat. Applying kaolinite clay (a natural mineral that can act as a sunburn preventive) can help reduce sun damage.

Now let's move from edible plants to some of my favorite ornamental species that add color and beauty to the garden.

→ *Pomegranate*

Elevate Your Space with Antique Roses

What exactly are antique roses? Antique roses are varieties that existed prior to 1867. This year marks when hybrid tea roses, those that were intentionally hybridized over generations, came into existence. To simplify, antique roses belong to a class that existed before the first modern hybrid rose. They are also known as "heirloom" or "old garden" roses. They are prized for their hardiness, disease resistance, and prominent growth. They are some of my favorite roses to grow in the garden.

↑ *An illustration of my 'Peggy Martin' rose arch in bloom*

INCORPORATING A ROSE ARCH

While having roses around my garden is a beautiful addition, one thing I did to further brighten the space was create my 'Peggy Martin' rose arch. Making this decision was one small step in changing the overall tone of my garden, sending it from average to amazing! We will discuss this process in further detail on the coming pages but let us first discuss the history behind this awe-inspiring rose.

← *An enjoyable day in the garden under my 'Peggy Martin' rose arch*

A HISTORY OF THE 'PEGGY MARTIN' ROSE

The 'Peggy Martin' rose survived for two weeks under twenty feet (6 m) of Hurricane Katrina's salt water. It was one of only two plants left standing in the garden of Mrs. Peggy Martin of Plaquemines Parish, Louisiana. Ever since growers revived and propagated 'Peggy Martin' cuttings, the rose has become a symbol of resilience, regrowth, and survival for gardeners across the Gulf Coast. The 'Peggy Martin' rose is known as the "Gem of The South" and "the Hurricane Katrina Rose." My 'Peggy Martin' rose arch is my pride and joy and my favorite area of the garden!

'Peggy Martin's' impressive resilience and beautiful pink blooming flowers will easily transform your garden into a remarkable sight. A robust spring- and fall-blooming climber, 'Peggy Martin' is thornless and hardy in USDA zones 5 to 11.

CREATING MY 'PEGGY MARTIN' ROSE ARCH

While I am extremely proud of how gorgeous my 'Peggy Martin' rose arch looks, it was surprisingly easy to build. I bought an iron trellis with ornate scrolling and a decorative fleur-de-lis on top. Since roses can get quite heavy, I stabilized the trellis with leftover rebar stakes. I bought two, three-gallon (11 L) 'Peggy Martin' roses and planted one on each side of the trellis.

You can choose many forms of trellises. A basic trellis serves as a screen or as support for climbing plants. Examples include pergolas, bamboo trellises, cattle panel arches, wrought iron arbors, or any garden support structure.

Once the roses are planted, the real fun begins! As the roses grow in the spring, I gently weave the new shoots through the trellis. I check on my 'Peggy Martins' every week to see if I need to weave any new shoots in. I don't weave older,

thicker canes into the trellis because they are brittle and snap off more easily. If you break a few, don't fret! New shoots are sure to regenerate. Once the canes reach the top, I simply continue to weave the shoots down the other side. Once you have the shape you desire, you can prune your roses to maintain the shape.

During spring and early fall, I like to apply a three-in-one product to keep my roses healthy. This product from my local garden center includes fertilizer and insect and disease control. I also apply at least a three-inch-thick (7.5 cm) layer of mulch. To deter any overwintering spores or pests, you can apply a dormant oil spray during the winter.

Another way I keep my roses happy in the summer is to prune off the diseased stems and leaves. 'Peggy Martin' roses are pruned a bit differently from other roses.

↑ *The best technique for weaving a rose cane onto an arch*

↑ My 'Peggy Martin' rose arch in full spring bloom

HELPFUL TIPS FOR PRUNING 'PEGGY MARTIN' ROSES

1. Prune the canes immediately after blooming, heavily in spring, and lightly in the fall. Pruning controls the shape and size of your plant and encourages more prolific growth and blooming.

2. Cut stems at a forty-five-degree angle so water runs off the branches. This discourages rot.

3. Remove any diseased canes, as these can be entry points for other pathogens and insect infestation.

4. Never prune more than one third to one half of the plant at a time. Severe pruning can deter blooming and possibly kill the plant.

5. Don't prune in the fall; this allows the plant to harden off for winter.

6. In late winter, remove dead canes to direct the plant's energy towards live canes, prevent disease and encourage new growth.

My 'Peggy Martins' are planted in a sunny location with well-drained soil. This is imperative if you want fast growth and blooms. I use a drip watering system (also throughout my gardens) to prevent disease and save water. While 'Peggy Martin' is very disease- and pest-resistant, overhead watering wets the leaves, which can cause fungal disease, especially in summer's heat and humidity.

GENERAL ROSE CARE

Plant your roses in a sunny, well drained location. As they mature, roses will bloom more prolifically with each year.

It's always best to address any problems as soon as you notice them. Remove all diseased or infested stems, as well as fallen leaves around the plant base. In summer, *lightly* prune diseased stems and leaves only in dry weather. In spring, summer, and fall, apply a curative fungicide to your roses. As mentioned earlier, be sure to spray your roses with a dormant oil spray to address any overwintering spores.

In spring, you should see new growth. As I do with my 'Peggy Martin' rose, I fertilize all my roses twice a year, in spring and fall, with a three-in-one product that includes a fertilizer, a fungicide, and an insecticide. Used in the spring, it prevents funguses. Always aim to prevent problems before they worsen.

↑ *'Belinda's Dream' is a fast-growing shrub rose, a cross between 'Tiffany' and 'Jersey Beauty', and it's a favorite rose in the garden.*

↑ *'Awakening' is another favorite in the garden. This modern climbing rose is a sport of 'New Dawn', but with twice as many petals.*

Seasonal Gardening at Southern Home and Farm

Here in the southern United States, we're fortunate to enjoy multiple growing seasons, so we can grow an array of plants nearly year-round. The warm climate and regular rainfall in the South enable a variety of crops several times a year. Southern gardeners can enjoy fresh produce and beautiful blooms for many months.

The two most prominent growing seasons in the South are spring and fall. These seasons' milder temperatures provide near perfect conditions for a wide range of plants, from vegetables to flowers. Each season offers unique planting opportunities.

To help visualize and plan for each season, I've included two illustrated layouts of my garden, one tailored for spring and another for fall. These layouts aim to maximize growth and keep the garden productive and beautiful all season long.

MY SPRING GARDEN

Let's begin with the layout of my spring garden. The orientation is true north. Starting from the right-hand side, you will see an exterior gate, along with the split rail cedar fence encircling the entire garden. The walkways are lined with decomposed granite. On the outer perimeter

we planted about thirty antique roses, each one labeled.

Past the rose arch you will see two beds of herbs on the left and right. These are always filled with a bit of color, as well as some seasonal herbs (see page 48 for some of my favorites).

Just beyond these beds, you find our water feature: a petrified wood disappearing fountain. It has an underground reservoir and a recirculating pump, both covered at the base with river rock. Water moves through the stone via a PVC pipe that was cored into the middle of the stone. To keep the water fountain free from algae, non-harmful, environmentally friendly additives are mixed in with the water seasonally. We also add a calcium preventive to keep the stone free of build-up.

↑ *The layout of my spring garden*

↑ *A large chicken wire cloche safeguards my strawberry plants.*

We typically plant varieties of peppers and tomatoes in the two beds just beyond the water feature. I rotate these crops annually to ensure healthy plants and soil (see Crop Rotation, page 30). The remaining beds are filled with seasonal vegetables. Asparagus has found its permanent home in the corner of the southwest bed. Between these two beds, we built another arbor to mirror the rose arch. To create this, we took a twenty foot (6 m) piece of cattle panel from a farm supply store and gently bent it, attaching it to four garden stakes (one on each corner) with zip ties. I planted trumpet honeysuckle vine here and weaved the vine throughout the arbor as it grew. Honeysuckle vine attracts amazing pollinators, including our family favorite, the beautiful hummingbird! (See Chapter 8 for more information on this process.)

On the south side of the garden, you find three smaller exterior beds. The southwest bed is usually filled with squash and cucumbers in the spring. The center bed is a raised metal bed that matches the paint color of my tool shed and greenhouse, a creamy white. We usually fill this bed with colorful flowers, no matter the season. In the spring, you often find gerbera daisies, petunias, violas, and creeping Jenny growing there. In the summer, you find zinnias, angelonia, and dichondra. I love to incorporate trailing plants for a cascading effect down the sides and front of the raised bed container. With our climate, for the most part, these plants flower for many months.

Lastly, the southeast external bed usually has varieties of garlic, shallots, and onions, and strawberry pots are located near the raised bed container area and elsewhere nearby. I always use wire cloches atop the strawberries and new transplants to keep pesky garden critters away.

MY AUTUMN GARDEN

In the autumn, my garden plan is slightly different to accommodate seasonal vegetable varieties and flowers. After walking through the rose arch, which blooms less vigorously in the fall, you once again see two beds of herbs on the left and right. As in the spring, these are filled with a bit of color, as well as some seasonal herbs. A few of my favorites include lemon balm, thyme, rosemary, parsley, sage, comfrey, and coriander.

As you continue through the garden, you again see our water feature. The water feature still needs additives but less frequently.

I always sprinkle colorful flowers around the vegetable beds and down both sides of all beds. My favorite cool season flower is sweet alyssum; it's perfect for borders. The tiny, honey-scented white blossoms add a splash of brightness to my fall garden and always remind me of snow, something we rarely see this far south.

I fill the two beds just beyond the water feature with numerous fall vegetables including spinach, Swiss chard, lettuce (including 'Red Sails', buttercrunch, and romaine), mustard greens, spinach, cauliflower (including 'Cheddar', white, and purple), tomatoes, onions, and turnips. I once again rotate those crops annually to balance soil nutrients. The remaining two beds on the west side grow asparagus and extra veggies that may not fit into the middle beds. The trumpet honeysuckle vine on the back arch remains dormant during this time but will flush again in the spring.

↑ *The layout of my fall garden*

↑ *A serene view of our autumn garden*

In the fall, winter squash thrives in three exterior beds on the south side, just outside the double-loop ornamental wire fencing. This time of year, I love to use seasonal colors in the creamy white center bed. I plant snapdragons in the back, pentas, calendula, and dianthus, and finish with such trailing plants such as dichondra. In the winter, I fill this bed with paperwhite bulbs that soon emerge with the most fragrant blossoms. Lastly, the southeast external bed usually has varieties of Brussels sprouts and broccoli.

↑ *Lettuce bed with purple snapdragons and white alyssum*

Features to Fawn Over

Let's explore some different garden features that can help personalize your garden and add elements of your style and personality.

WATER FEATURES

Besides being pretty, water features provide crucial water sources for birds and pollinators.

Pollinators rely on three key things for survival: colorful plants for food (nectar and pollen), a suitable habitat, and a water source. If you provide these elements, they will come!

Adding water sources can be as easy as setting out small porcelain cups for thirsty pollinators.

Further efforts include installing water fountains and even small ponds. When choosing a water feature, consider your personal style; for a more traditional style, a small pond or classic fountain works well to reflect tradition. If you like modern, formal, or geometric fountain designs, choose reflecting ponds.

Fountains come in a variety of colors and materials to suit different styles. For our vintage garden, we chose a more natural-looking fountain made of petrified wood. The water gently trickles down and recirculates back to the top. We installed an automatic fill valve for ease of filling, and a float to stop the process once the basin is filled. A PVC pipe cored in the center recirculates the water. I covered the mechanics with river rock for the natural look.

Small ponds can be charming accents to the garden, too. At a former residence, we installed a small pond underneath an arbor filled with jasmine. We stocked the pond with Koi fish and added water garden plants: water lilies, mosaic flowers, cattails, and water hyacinths.

ALGAE CONTROL

Be aware that algae can form in fountains in full sun. You can add environmentally safe algae control to prevent it.

↑ *A close-up view of the top of our fountain*

↑ *Our garden's petrified wood water feature is framed beautifully by the garden arch.*

ARCHWAYS, ARBORS, AND GATES, OH MY

The entrance to your garden sets the tone for your entire space. It welcomes visitors and tells a story. An intriguing entry sparks visitors' curiosity to explore what lies beyond. A show-stopping entryway can take your garden to the next level. I planted my beautiful 'Peggy Martin' rose on a metal arbor at the entrance of my garden, and she never disappoints! My twelve-foot (3.5 m) arbor explodes with beautiful pink blossoms every spring and fall. Accented by a pair of vintage wooden shutters, it makes the most gorgeous entrance to my garden.

You can buy metal arches or make your own using your garden's natural materials. Gather stems and wire and supports such as wood, garden stakes or even stones. The latter is an ideal option for cottage gardens. If you favor a more contemporary style, metal structures work better.

PLANTS TO CONSIDER FOR ARCHES AND ARBORS

For *shaded and partially shaded* locations: Opt for rapidly growing vines like Virginia creeper (also known as American ivy), and Boston ivy; non-invasive Carolina jessamine, climbing hydrangea, and passionflower.

For *sunny* locations: Choose blooming climbers such as mandevilla, jasmine, clematis, wisteria, and, of course, my favorites: trumpet honeysuckle vines and climbing roses.

ART WITHIN THE GARDEN

I enjoy placing vintage pieces in the garden to heighten the ambiance. They add the finishing touches! Let's explore how you can do the same. You'll find much more inspiration for using art and vintage finds in the coming chapters, too.

← Handmade ceramic mushrooms enchant my shade garden. Their vibrant glazed porcelain caps sway gently in the breeze. Blue, green, and brown hues bring a fairy-like quality to this space.

↑ I also placed a handwoven bee house in my shade garden, a cozy home for our pollinator friends. Made of palm, it adds a delightful touch of vintage charm to this space, and a colorful focal point.

↑ *I also use tools as art accents. I display three large antique farm and garden tools on the side of the farmhouse facing the garden. I also hung a vintage garden sign just above these tools. Viewed through my rose arbor, they create the most picturesque scene in the garden.*

The Greenhouse

Outbuildings—such as our greenhouse, tool shed, and grain silo—are another way to add interest and beauty to your space. Their functionality is another definite bonus. We added a ten-foot by sixteen-foot (3 by 5 m) greenhouse to our garden, and it has become a place of pride. We first poured a concrete slab, installed plumbing (including a commercial sink and sprayer), a floor drain, and electricity (including fluorescent lights and a chandelier for ambiance). We then built our customized greenhouse with a kit and painted it to match the farmhouse.

I am very proud of all that hard work. After I painted, stenciled, and sealed my floor (see page 70), we placed a twelve foot long (3.6 m) vintage merchant table along one side of the greenhouse as a working surface. On the other side are

coated wire racks from a restaurant supply store used for storing plants, seedlings, transplants, and other garden wares.

We then added a matching tool shed painted the same colors as the farmhouse and greenhouse.

We added more wire racks for storage space along with utility hooks for hanging garden tools.

ENHANCING YOUR GREENHOUSE

There are many ways to personalize a greenhouse. I'll share some tips for decorating your greenhouse indoors and out. Let's delve into the specifics of how I stenciled the greenhouse floor.

DIY Stenciling Your Floor

When the chance came to build the ultimate greenhouse, I jumped at it! I was determined to get every detail perfect, including creating a focal point on the floor. I had previously seen stenciled flooring, and was eager to give it a try myself. This was my first time stenciling such a large area, and I could not be more thrilled with how it turned out!

MATERIALS NEEDED:

- Porch and patio floor paint (two contrasting colors)
- Paint tray
- Stencils
- Paint roller
- Two 9" (5 x 23 cm) foam rollers with ½" (1 cm) nap
- One 9" (23 cm) foam roller with a ¾9" (5 mm) nap
- Paint roller extension pole
- Blue painter's tape
- Matte concrete sealer spray

↑ *The greenhouse floor prior to starting the project*

STEP 1:

The concrete pad had to cure for thirty days. *Curing* is a crucial process to give the concrete time to set and harden properly, making it more resistant to cracking and drying out. After it was cured, I power-washed the concrete to thoroughly clean it, allowing it to dry completely afterward. A clean floor makes painting far easier. After drying, I lightly swept any residue off the floor to ensure it was spotless before painting. Then I used a specialized slate gray paint on the floor. I stenciled the floor with white paint, a striking contrast that draws attention to the design.

Pro Tip

A smooth finish paint works best on concrete.

STEP 2:

I bought four large stencil patterns, then taped them together to save time rolling. I began in the center of the room, around the greenhouse drain, and painted one section at a time. After completing a section, I moved the taped stencil pattern first above, then below, allowing each section to dry before returning to it. I repeated this process consistently, moving back and forth, which allowed each section to dry while I worked on the next one.

← *The greenhouse floor after being stenciled and sealed*

↑ *My first attempt at stenciling a floor!*

Pro Tip

Be careful not to work too quickly or use too much paint, as it can seep under the stencil, blurring the design. I didn't mind this when it happened, as it added to the vintage charm.

↑ *Nothing beats the look of a freshly painted greenhouse floor.*

STEP 3:

I finished by spraying the floor with a clear, matte-finish concrete sealer for a vintage feel. A shiny floor would not fit the look I wanted; it could also be slippery when wet. After spraying on the sealant, I used a clean roller with a ³⁄₁₆" (5 mm) nap to smooth out any bubbles. I used an extension pole for this so I could stand upright. Once the sealing was done, I installed wire racks to store my plants, seedlings, and transplants.

STEP 4:

I added a chandelier for eye-catching glamour, along with vintage shutters flanking the Dutch doors, and a 12-foot (3.6 m) long vintage mercantile table for a work surface, and an antique seed cabinet for extra storage, workspace, and decorative charm.

Stenciling was a lengthy process requiring patience, but so worth it. I highly encourage you to try it, perhaps with a smaller project. Stenciling transforms any space. It looks amazing on porch floors, stair risers, and even on mudroom floors.

Stenciling can turn ordinary areas into dazzling spaces. With creativity and vision, the possibilities are endless!

IDYLLIC INTERIOR: DECORATING THE INSIDE OF YOUR GREENHOUSE

For each season, I love to decorate the greenhouse, farmhouse table, and our metal grain silo. People tell me my greenhouse can't possibly be functional because it's "too fancy." I disagree! I practically live in that space, so why not go all out and decorate a place that brings me so much joy?

We painted the interior to match the outside with a custom color that also matches the farmhouse. If you want a custom color, try color matching apps, which can match the paint in any photo. They're easy to use and free!

Besides being functional, I wanted my greenhouse to evoke a sense of charm. Vintage pieces inside radiate charm. The narrow vintage mercantile table doubles as a decorative space beneath the windows but also is a workspace, which I use to repot, plant seeds, or transplant. I decorate the windows seasonally as well as the back of the table.

I am always on the lookout for interesting and unique items. I found two pairs of vintage shutters while traveling to Alabama, proof you should never pass up antique stores. I painted them a dark brown color and then with a fresh coat of creamy white paint. Next, I spot sanded them to let the original dark paint peek through to create a weathered, old world aesthetic. I often hang decorative ornaments on them, like brightly colored strings of hearts.

The greenhouse measures sixteen feet (5 m). Since the mercantile table isn't that long, I had a few extra feet. To fill it, I bought a gorgeous pale

↑ *A pale blue vintage plate rack sits in the greenhouse, displaying pots and plants.*

↑ *My vintage mercantile table in the greenhouse is decorated for the Fourth of July.*

← Vintage shutters inside the greenhouse adorned with quilted strings of hearts

blue vintage wire rack on the way to Fredericksburg, Texas, the most charming and idyllic town. I placed this rack at an angle at the end of the table. It has shelving and lots of hooks for storage. It also makes a great hot cocoa bar in the winter.

As with gardening, think vertically when decorating, too. I love to decorate the ceiling of the greenhouse. We recently had a tropical storm pass directly over the farm. We had damage but were fortunate, compared to some. I decided to turn the situation into something positive and focused on creating a centerpiece for my greenhouse ceiling. I gathered enough large fallen branches from around the farm to span the length of my greenhouse, then I trimmed the branches to create more space between the smaller stems.

I then hung the branches with wire, eye hooks, and small carabiners across the ceiling, paying careful attention to arrange the stems around the chandelier. Once in place, I decorated the ceiling with long, flowing faux wisteria blossoms. When both Dutch doors are open, the cross breeze gently sways the white blossoms, making for a serene and soothing atmosphere.

Creating a DIY Ceiling of Flowers

MATERIALS NEEDED:

- Fallen branches of various sizes
- Wire
- Eye hooks
- Small carabiners
- Faux white wisteria blossoms

STEP 1:
I collected my branches around the farm after a storm.

STEP 2:
Next, I installed eye hooks in the ceiling to hang the branches across the length of the ceiling.

STEP 3:
I draped faux wisteria blossoms over the branches, from one end of the ceiling to the other. The branches naturally hang at different heights, so the blossoms followed suit, creating a natural look.

*Fallen branches from the farm
adorned with white wisteria blossoms*

THE PERFECT PERIMETER: DECORATING THE OUTSIDE OF YOUR GREENHOUSE

I use all "real estate" available and so decorate the outside of the greenhouse, too. We decorate the eaves at Christmastime with garlands and lights, and the doors get wreaths or sprays. In the summer, even the upper metal siding is used to hang flags. For Memorial Day and July Fourth, I hang bunting on the outside of the grain silo and greenhouse. Just another way to decorate those spaces while celebrating the season! I use simple eye hooks to hang the bunting on the greenhouse and zip ties on the silo.

I also use some space outside the greenhouse for my outdoor potting bench. It's just another spot to pot my favorite plants and store my many topiaries and smaller garden tools.

I was so excited to build custom outdoor shelving outside the greenhouse this year! We painted the shelving to match the greenhouse for a seamless look. The shelving is easy to remove in the off season.

↑ *Bunting draped from the greenhouse*

↑ *Side view of greenhouse with fall pumpkin shelving*

I've always dreamed of creating a pumpkin display. For fall, I festooned the shelves with shredded wood excelsior for festive charm, then topped it with pumpkins. I also included simple vintage fall signs, like "Gourds," "Hay Bales," and, of course, "Pumpkins."

I decorate this shelving for Christmas as well. I line the shelves with beautiful red poinsettias in gold foil liners. This colorful look (which I discuss further in chapter 3) creates a truly stunning visual effect.

Autumn front view of the greenhouse

Front view of the greenhouse at Christmas with poinsettia-filled shelving

CREATE YOUR VISION GALLERY

Inspiration from my garden you can use to create your own outdoor oasis and transform your garden space into a sanctuary.

↑ *Potting bench*

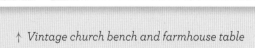

↑ *Vintage church bench and farmhouse table*

→ *Small garden tools for precision work*

↑ *Obelisk
with bleeding
heart vine*

← *Both garden arches—trumpet
honeysuckle in front and a
'Peggy Martin' rose in the back*

Dream in Color
Vibrant flowers for the farmhouse garden

View the garden as your canvas. The flowers and plants you choose are the paints that bring it to life. Blending colors in harmony creates a symphony of color that transforms the space into an ideal garden sanctuary. Let's explore the colorful world of flowers and plants, learning how to choose, combine, and care for them while cultivating a garden that bursts with life and energy. Implementing color within your garden offers a range of benefits that surpass aesthetics.

The Benefits of Incorporating a Variety of Colors

1. AESTHETIC APPEAL

It goes without saying that adding color provides aesthetic appeal. Colorful plants and flowers create a visually interesting landscape that enhances the beauty of your outdoor space. Designing your garden with colors that flow in harmony provides curb appeal and makes your space more attractive. However, aesthetics is not just a positive influence in your garden, it also gives you an outlet for your creativity. Your choice of colors reflects your personal taste and style. Whether you prefer bold, vibrant colors or soft, light pastels, your garden is a canvas for self-expression.

2. EMOTIONAL AND PSYCHOLOGICAL HEALTH

Different colors evoke different emotions. For example, warm, bright colors can brighten your mood and cultivate a sense of happiness. On the other hand, cool, muted colors can promote a sense of relaxation and calm. Surrounding yourself with vibrant foliage has been proven to reduce stress levels. Gardening itself therapeutically benefits overall mental health.

3. ATTRACTING WILDLIFE

Colorful plants attract all kinds of wildlife to your garden. Pollinators love brightly colored flowers. Sunflowers and honeysuckle vines attract seed-eating birds, butterflies, and hummingbirds, my personal favorite visitor. Pollinators provide the garden with natural pest control and encourage a balanced ecosystem, vital roles in the garden's health and productivity. They are always welcome!

4. CREATIVE LANDSCAPING

You can use color in your garden in contrasting ways or monochromatic looks. Zinnias come in many bright colors, so I put a lot of them in my summer zinnia bed for a beautiful pop of color in summer's palette. Bright colors also draw the eye to specific areas of your garden. You can design colors in a pattern that creates a visual flow within the garden.

↑ *A side view of the silo entrance, with vibrant petunias and salvia, welcoming guests*

5. SEASONAL COLOR

With your own garden, you get to change up your landscape throughout the year. By the end of the fall, when certain plants have stopped growing, you can simply replace them with vibrant options that last throughout the winter. Having a continuous display of color ensures that your garden maintains its beauty and interest year-round. Cold-climate gardeners with gardens that go dormant in the winter should consider adding dwarf evergreens, shrubs with berries, and other plants that provide winter interest to the garden.

6. ENCOURAGE TIME SPENT OUTDOORS

Having a vibrant garden just outside your door invites you to spend more time outdoors. When you step outside, you can garden, read on a bench, or socialize with friends and family. All this outdoor time boosts your mood and creativity, improves mental health, and reduces stress. What is not to like?

7. EDUCATIONAL OPPORTUNITIES

You can learn a lot through gardening, about different plants, their growth habits, and their interactions with the environment. A colorful garden also provides a great opportunity to teach your children about gardening, pollinators, and plant maintenance in a way that is interesting and engaging to them!

→ *A close-up of my metal raised bed just outside the silo entrance, where wisteria is greening up for spring. The base contains brightly colored petunias, creeping Jenny, and dichondra, with purple sage and more petunias nestled just below.*

The Language of Color in the Garden

As mentioned, color has more value than aesthetics. Color establishes moods and feelings and creates garden themes. Think of color in the garden as an extension of your interior space. Do you love colorful spaces or is your home more neutral in tone? Maybe you prefer subtle pops of color as accents. You can create a seamless look from indoors to outdoors when you extend your indoor color palette to your outdoor areas.

Simple color schemes to try in your garden include monochromatic and color blocking.

- A *monochromatic* color scheme refers to different hues (varieties) of one color. Examples here include all shades of pink or all shades of blue.
- *Color blocking* is simply the use of opposites on the color wheel. In the garden, I use contrasting colors for maximum visual impact, especially in spring and summer. Examples here include the use of red and green or blue and yellow. If you are not familiar with a color wheel, it easily outlines color theory. They are very inexpensive and free online.

Next, let's discuss the language of color in your garden.

RED
Red is a bold color, evoking powerful psychological responses. Red flowers include geraniums, zinnias, and dahlias. Red crops include red bell peppers, tomatoes, and Swiss chard.

ORANGE
Orange evokes a sense of energy and cheerfulness, which brings a bright and playful feel to the garden. It combines the happiness of yellow with the vibrancy of red. Orange flowers include marigolds, zinnias, and calendula. Orange crops include 'Orange Wellington' tomatoes, 'Cheddar' cauliflower, and butternut squash.

YELLOW
Yellow is one of the brightest colors, so it makes sense that it symbolizes happiness, encouragement, and optimism. Yellow in your garden yields a positive atmosphere. Yellow flowers include coreopsis, sunflowers, and yellow tulips. Yellow crops include yellow squash, corn, and golden zucchini.

GREEN

Green represents renewal, new growth, and freshness, everything a garden naturally embodies! Green backdrop tones make all other colors pop. Green flowers include 'Limelight' hydrangeas, hellebore, chrysanthemums, zinnias, and celosia. Green crops include mustard greens, broccoli, asparagus, okra, and chives.

BLUE/PURPLE

Both blue and purple evoke tranquility, wellness, calmness, and relaxation. Blue and purple flowers include hydrangeas, lavender, and delphiniums. Blue crops include blue corn, blue kale, and blue potatoes.

PINK

Pink is one of the softest colors and is very popular in gardening. Its softness conveys a sense of femininity, and in some cases, romanticism. Pink can be both calming and refreshing, depending on the shade chosen. As a complementary color, it adds a splash of fun! Pink flowers include 'Peggy Martin' rose (my personal favorite), snapdragons, zinnia, and vinca. Pink crops include rhubarb, pink Swiss chard, and pink tomatoes.

The Influence and Effect of Colors

Consider how colors can influence your plantings, as they establish the tone and mood of your garden. Let's explore two different color palettes.

COOL COLORS

Cool colors like green, blue, and purple, create a sense of relaxation and calm. In plantings, these colors recede. These pairings make your space appear larger. Examples in this color palette include angelonia, dianthus, hydrangeas, lavender, pansies, petunias, and salvia.

WARM COLORS

Warm colors include shades of red, orange, and yellow. These colors often appear to move forward visually and stand out. Place these plantings in spaces that might otherwise go unnoticed. You can also use these colors to highlight spaces where you want to draw attention. Warm color flowers include calendula, daffodils, portulaca, sunflowers, zinnias, and tuberous begonias.

↑ *Pink zinnias from the metal raised bed*

↑ *My metal raised bed in spring filled with snapdragons, gerbera daisies, violas, and creeping Jenny*

The Best Colorful Flowers to Plant in Your Farmhouse Garden

I enjoy adding bright and vibrant flowers to my garden every season. Since much of my garden receives full sun, I plant many sun-loving annuals and perennials. Keep in mind my gardening zone is 9a, so your plant choices might differ from mine. A local specialty nursery can help you choose the best options for your zone.

Now, let's take a closer look at how I seasonally redesign and plant my raised metal bed to celebrate changing weather and bloom cycles. From early spring freshness to the rich hues of autumn, these seasonal plantings make for a flourishing garden year-round.

SPRING

In spring, I love to plant blooms to brighten up the garden like violas, petunias, blue sage, snapdragons, and stock, just to name a few. Violas add cheerful blossoms in a wide range of colors. Violas perform well in the cooler spring temperatures. Petunias spill over the edges of planters and raised beds with their cascading waves of color. Blue sage sends up beautiful spikes of deep blue flowers that attract bees and butterflies. Snapdragons add vertical interest with tall stems and interesting blooms, while stock fills the air with its lovely, sweet fragrance and provides clusters of bright flowers.

SUMMER

In the summer, my garden is filled with staple flowers that thrive in the warm weather. Vinca adds bright pops of color and endures well in summer heat. Begonias are another favorite for their lush foliage and vibrant flowers in many colors. Angelonia brings an airy texture and height to the garden with its tall spikes of tiny, orchid-like blossoms, while the zinnias burst with color into the frame, offering a long bloom time and attracting many pollinators. All combined, it creates a lively, robust summer garden full of life and color.

↑ *My metal bed in summer filled with zinnias, begonias, vinca, creeping Jenny, and dichondra*

Pro Tip

Try the 'Profusion' variety of zinnias. This variety is not only long-lasting but mildew resistant, very helpful as zinnias are prone to fungal disease.

AUTUMN

In autumn, I like planting snapdragons, calendula, and dianthus for their vibrant blooms and seasonal charm. Snapdragons give height to any bed or container and come in an array of colors, while calendula adds a warm, golden hue that brightens up any garden space. Although dianthus is known for its delicate, jagged-edge blooms, keep in mind that all varieties of dianthus are toxic to pets. If you have furry friends that like to roam in the garden, plant these with caution to ensure your pets' safety.

↑ A fall look at my metal raised bed filled with calendula, dianthus, and dichondra

Winter is the perfect time to plant sweet alyssum, cyclamen, poinsettias, and paperwhites if you live in a warm climate like mine. I like to plant my garden from the shortest to the tallest plants, which provides depth and develops interesting views in the garden. To enhance the garden's overall appeal, I combine annuals with perennials. The annuals change season after season, but the perennials give the garden a constant backbone that flourishes for years. Some of my favorite perennials include dwarf yaupon, wisteria, foxtail ferns, Indian hawthorn, and several species of native grasses. Of course, any annuals that reseed will come up again next year. And if they do, let them grow. These self-sowing plants will keep appearing, and you will be able to enjoy a magnificent display of blooms that nature continually reintroduces into your garden.

The winter season holds a special place in my heart. This is the time when I plant sweet alyssum. As I mentioned in an earlier chapter, this delicate flower, with its tiny, clustered blooms, always reminds me of a light dusting of snow, a rare and magical sight in the southern region. Its crisp, white appearance brings a touch of winter wonder to the garden. This is one of the reasons sweet alyssum has become one of my favorite cool-season flowers. Versatile alyssum is perfect for planting along the edges of garden beds, where it gently spills over, softening the borders and adding a natural, flowing look. Planted along walkways, it creates a welcoming, fragrant path that invites you into the garden. Not only does it add visual interest and texture to the landscape, but its subtle honey-like scent also fills the air, making time spent outdoors even more enjoyable. This cascading beauty truly transforms the garden into a tranquil winter retreat.

↑ *Winter view of my metal raised bed filled with poinsettias, dichondra, and creeping Jenny*

Color in the Shade

In my cozy, shaded garden, I love infusing vibrant splashes of color by planting annuals such as impatiens, which provide cheerful pinks, reds, and whites, and blue daze, with its striking blue blooms that brighten even the shadiest corners. I also rely on perennials. Among these, hostas hold a special place, particularly the 'Guacamole' variety, which captivates with its lime green foliage edged in deep green. The bold leaves add texture and interest throughout the growing season. I also plant a variety of ferns with delicate, feathery fronds, adding a graceful, woodland feel to the space. These carefully chosen plants blend to make my shaded garden a lively space year-round.

Caladiums make an outstanding addition to any shade garden, with some varieties, like strap leaf caladiums, even tolerating sunlight. These plants grow from bulbs and should be planted when the temperature consistently reaches around 60°F (16°C) for optimal growth. Caladiums are known for their vibrant array of colors, showcasing shades of red, pink, burgundy, green, white, and various striking multicolored patterns. To create a truly captivating and dramatic visual impact, consider planting caladiums in large, clustered groups.

Pro Tip

Caladiums do not like wet feet so be sure not to overwater! Remove any brown leaves to encourage fresh, healthy growth throughout the season.

All these plants are low maintenance and bring remarkable visual appeal to any garden. Their easy-care nature combined with their vibrant and lush presence make them perfect for enhancing the beauty of outdoor spaces.

A Vibrant Garden

Colorful flora and foliage are the key to cultivating a vibrant, inviting garden. Through the careful selection of these plants, you can create a visually stunning space. There are many benefits to curating a vibrant garden space. Not only will you feel accomplished, but you will feel creatively fulfilled. Whether you prefer the soft pastels of spring, the vibrant hues of summer, or the warm, rich tones of fall, there is a world of color waiting to be planted!

↑ *Sweet alyssum 'Snow Princess', shown here in my raised garden bed alongside dianthus, is a heat-tolerant variety with a honey-like fragrance and delicate white blooms.*

CREATE YOUR VISION GALLERY

Inspiration from my garden to help you dream in color and infuse your garden with many colorful hues.

↑ 'Indigo Cherry' tomatoes

↑ Colorful zinnias

→ Zinnias and rose arch

↑ *Colorful petunias*

↑ *Closeup of spring bed with color*

↑ *Silo with petunias*

↑ *Petunias in stone container*

Living Décor

Decorating and designing with plants, flowers, and vegetables

Living décor brings life and movement, enhancing both indoor and outdoor areas with organic charm. Living plants beautify your space and foster a sense of calm and connection with nature. Whether you're using lush foliage, cascading vines, or blooming flowers, living décor transforms your surroundings into a lively and welcoming space. Let's explore how you can achieve this look by incorporating elements straight from your garden to create an eye-catching natural masterpiece.

Floral Arrangements

Floral arrangements offer a timeless way to enhance and enrich your décor, indoors and out. Floral arrangements infuse a space with color, texture, and a sense of liveliness that few other design elements can match. They have the unique ability to complement the ambiance and enhance the overall mood, making any space feel more inviting and refined. By choosing seasonal blooms, you can keep your décor in tune with nature, introducing a fresh and dynamic aesthetic that evolves throughout the year. Whether it's the bright, cheerful tones of spring tulips, the warm, rich hues of autumn chrysanthemums, or the delicate whites of winter amaryllis, seasonal flowers help establish an immediate connection with the time of year. This not only brings visual interest but also engages the senses and evokes emotions tied to different seasons. Ultimately, floral arrangements serve as living art that can transform an ordinary space into a sophisticated and harmonious environment.

Adding fresh flowers, greenery, wildflowers, or even grasses to a floral arrangement or tablescape brings a pleasing pop of freshness to your table. These natural elements create a warm and friendly feel that are sure to welcome friends and family.

If you are new to floral design, start with a freshly cleaned container filled with a piece of coated chicken wire shaped into a ball to hold the stems and make it easier to place them. Or crisscross the top of your container with floral tape. Finish by encircling the rim with a final piece of tape to secure the grid. More seasoned designers can start by crisscrossing their greenery in their hands, then placing them in the container. The matrix of greens secures the floral stems like a "floral frog." Make a fresh cut at the base of each stem at a 45-degree angle with a clean knife. This exposes more surface area for the flowers and foliage to take up water. Always remove any foliage that's below the water line to deter rot and bacteria.

Fill your container with lukewarm water and add floral food or a few drops of lemon or lime juice to deter bacteria. Be sure to change the water every few days and keep stems clean under the water line to deter bacterial growth.

I like to place my larger, focal flowers in the container first, then design around them using accent flowers. Be sure to face flowers outwards and use focal flowers in odd numbers. This looks more natural than a perfectly symmetrical arrangement. For a more cottage garden feel, I like to design arrangements asymmetrically with lots of dripping greenery around the neck of the vase.

My favorite types of greenery to use are lemon leaf and seeded eucalyptus. Get the latter, when possible, as seeded eucalyptus is only available seasonally and not during the warmer months. In addition to focal flowers, I add smaller sized flowers and taller stems to create dimension and texture. Lastly, I add filler flowers to fill in any open gaps in the arrangement.

↑ *For this Christmas season tabletop arrangement in the farmhouse, I surrounded vintage ornaments with fresh pepper berries.*

To keep your arrangement fresh, place it away from direct sunlight. Flowers wilt faster in strong lighting. A good, clean cut with a pair of sharp scissors or a knife removes about half an inch from the bottom of each stem and makes a world of difference to keep your floral display fresh and always looking its best.

Here are a few options to keep in mind when choosing various types of floral products for your designs:

FRESH FLOWERS

Fresh flowers enrich the aesthetic in any space, with a wide range of colors and subtle textures. Artificial flowers will not express the same touch of life.

Fresh flowers' light natural fragrance makes spaces more welcoming. Fresh flowers and greenery bring a touch of charm to any setting. Fresh flowers offer an experience that appeals to the senses and elevates the ambiance of your home and table.

I prefer to choose seasonal blooms for a natural and fresh aesthetic. When choosing fresh flowers, look for buds that are still healthy and intact, not drooping. Also choose flowers that have not fully opened. Those flowers will last longer.

Keep in mind that not all flowers are available year-round due to their natural growth cycles and seasonality. The availability of specific blooms can vary greatly depending on the time of year and regional climate conditions.

Pro Tip

To fully open fresh-cut roses, hold the stem gently between your hands with the bloom facing downward. Carefully twirl the stem back and forth between the palms of your hands. This technique encourages the petals to open, giving you beautifully fluffed, full blooms!

DRIED FLOWERS

Naturally *dried flowers* are often rigid and faded. However, there is a place for them in design. Dried flowers cost less than fresh and offer a natural appearance. Plus, you can keep them year-round.

Following several years working in fresh floral design, I managed the dried floral department at a local flower shop. Transitioning to dried flowers required mastering different techniques and mechanics unique to the art. Unlike fresh flowers, dried blooms are more rigid and less pliable, so handling them with extra care is essential to prevent damage. Floral paint can add vibrant color to any dried flower. You can buy these paints in a variety of colors and from online retailers or craft stores. I always finish a dried floral design by applying a light spray of clear sealant specifically designed for dried flowers. This helps preserve the arrangement, enhancing its longevity and durability so it can retain its beauty longer.

PRESERVED FLOWERS

Preserved flowers are chemically treated to maintain suppleness, color and longevity. They are easier to bend and manipulate for design purposes but are more expensive. If you are looking for a vibrant option to keep long term, preserved flowers are for you. I use them in the farmhouse as mantel pieces for small décor like sweetheart roses in mint julep cups with a pretty ribbon. Easy flowers to try preserving are lemon leaf hydrangeas. Their large heads take up space and just a bit of greenery accents them. Have fun here and use a variety of complementary colors and textures that otherwise are not available in fresh form.

FAUX FLOWERS

Faux flowers are artificial flowers meant to look real. They're made of silk, paper, plastic, etc. Faux flowers come in a range of price points. I highly recommend using higher quality florals that closely mimic the look and feel of real blooms.

↑ *I've combined both artificial and real greenery in my Christmas chandelier. Can you spot the faux pieces? When styled just right, they can trick even the keenest eye.*

Although pricier, they look far more natural. When mixed with organic florals, they trick the eye into believing they are one natural piece. The benefits here: Faux flowers are low maintenance, and you can reuse them year after year. Another advantage of using faux flowers is their year-round availability. This makes for practicality in busy households. Although I prefer fresh flowers, I'm not against using faux ones for the reasons mentioned above. I highly encourage you to give them a try, but make sure to blend them with fresh florals for a seamless appearance whenever possible.

Pro Tip

One of my all-time favorite tips: Mixing faux flowers with fresh flowers in your floral arrangements. Once fully arranged, it becomes difficult to tell the difference. It is also a great money-saving tip as the faux stems can be reused year after year for cost effectiveness.

This is also the time to experiment with bold colors and a variety of textures, which might not be achievable with fresh flowers due to seasonal availability.

DECORATIVE CONTAINERS

When designing your arrangements, think about unique and interesting containers. You can use most any object for dried, preserved, and faux arrangements. Think outside the box and use aged tins, old hat boxes, or even vintage fishing baskets. Containers can be modified to accommodate fresh flowers, if needed. Often you can place a container within a container to house the mechanics of your fresh floral arrangements. Think about using "containers" from the garden for an elevated look, such as hollowed-out fruits, gourds, and even pumpkins!

Let's take a closer look at the concept of using a pumpkin as a container in more detail. Keep in mind this arranging style can be applied to virtually any type of container.

Creating Your Own
Pumpkin Fall Arrangement

MATERIALS NEEDED:

- Pumpkin, any variety (I used a pink heirloom pumpkin here)
- Scissors and a sharp knife
- Floral foam
- Clear liner or vase
- Flowers (mums, roses, dahlias, fall leaves, stock, hydrangeas, berries, wheat, etc.) and greenery (seeded eucalyptus, lemon leaf, etc.) Forage your yard for colorful leaves, pine cones, and other flora.

Pro Tip

When choosing a pumpkin, pick one with a flat base so it sits securely. Make sure your pumpkin is sturdy and unblemished, free from deep scratches or soft spots. Those pumpkins last longer and make a better canvas for your floral arrangement.

← *Pumpkin floral arrangements*

STEP 1:

Carve the seeds and pulp out of your pumpkin. The sharp edge of a spoon is always a good scooping tool. Be sure to keep the seeds to bake for snacking!

Pro Tip

For the perfect fall snack with a nostalgic touch, try roasting your pumpkin seeds! First clean off the flesh from all seeds and then toss the seeds with olive oil or butter. Bake at 425°F (200°C) on a parchment-lined baking sheet for about fifteen minutes. Stir every few minutes to prevent burning. For a sweet and salty flavor, you can toss in honey, brown sugar, maple syrup, and salt. For a savory flavor, try adding grated cheese. If you would like to enhance the flavor with spices, wait until the seeds are fully baked to add. This prevents the spices from burning.

STEP 2:

Use your container to trace a matching line around the top of the pumpkin. This ensures a snug fit. Next, take your clear liner and fill it with wet floral foam that has been shaped to match the liner. Use floral tape to fasten the foam to the liner in a crisscross fashion. Be sure there is water in the liner, so the foam stays wet. Adding floral food to the water will make the arrangement last longer.

Pro Tip

To extend the life of your carved pumpkin, mix two tablespoons (30 ml) of bleach with two cups (470 ml) of water in a spray bottle. Lightly spray the inside of the pumpkin and allow it to dry. Then, seal the cut surfaces with petroleum jelly. If the pumpkin is for display only, use battery-operated candles instead of real candles.

STEP 3:

Design away! Here is where you can let your creativity shine. I like to add greenery first to create a base, then my focal flowers, followed by intermediate flowers. Then I fill in the gaps with filler flowers. Be sure to use a sharp knife and cut all stems at a 45-degree angle so the stem has more surface area to take up water. Rotate the arrangement so it looks nice on all sides. If you have a lazy Susan, use it! It makes it easier to move heavier arrangements.

Pro Tip

If you'd rather skip carving your pumpkin, there is an easy substitute. You can attach wet floral foam to the pumpkin's stem and build your arrangement right on top. Another option is to plant directly inside the pumpkin. Just hollow out half of the interior, fill it with soil, and add plants. As the pumpkin starts to decompose, you can plant it in your garden, where it naturally enriches the soil.

USING SUCCULENTS AS AN ALTERNATIVE ARRANGEMENT

Instead of flowers, you can use succulents. The process is simple. Start by spraying adhesive or hot glue to the top of a pumpkin. Press fresh moss down on the adhesive and add a variety of succulents. Varieties seen in the accompanying photo include crassula, echeveria, hens and chicks, kalanchoe, sedum, and string of pearls. Next, bind them with floral wire to keep them in place. Floral wire on a spool, with an easy cutter, works better than using individual wires. It is easier to control the specific length needed when wrapping the wire around the succulents. Once you have filled the top with succulents, add a spray of fall leaves and a bow. This creates a beautiful arrangement you can enjoy yourself or give as a thoughtful gift. The best thing here is that it will last all season long!

→ *Pumpkin succulent arrangement*

Topiaries

Topiaries are plants shaped through careful clipping and trimming or training into forms not seen in nature. Topiary designs range from simple shapes like spheres to elaborate animals or geometric patterns. The art of topiary dates to ancient Rome, a period I find fascinating for its ornamental horticulture and meticulously designed gardens. There is so much inspiration to draw from this era, and I encourage you to explore it further!

TYPES OF TOPIARY PLANTS

You can train most plants into topiaries, but some plants work better. When choosing topiary plants, look for small leaves, dense foliage, and compact growth. These characteristics are ideal for shaping or training. A few of my favorites include boxwood, eugenia, euonymus, ivy, angel vine, lavender, myrtle, Mexican heather, and rosemary.

If you want to decorate with larger topiaries, use plants such as boxwood, holly, juniper, pine, and privet. These plants are hardier in beds and are easy to shape.

TOPIARY SHAPES AND STYLES

Topiary designs range from geometric forms (globes, spheres, cones, spirals, pyramids) to whimsical animals. Spheres, "poodle" forms (two or three balls stacked vertically), and spirals are the most popular styles. Use your creativity here to form any shape you desire! You can train vining plants to grow into a circular or even a heart-shaped topiary.

TOPIARY PLACEMENT

You can put topiaries in small pots flanking a doorway or use them as focal points. Smaller potted topiaries always look best when grouped and displayed at different heights. A well-placed topiary can create the most fantastic effect in any space!

↑ *Part of my topiary collection showcased on the vintage seed cabinet in the greenhouse.*

TOPIARY CARE AND MAINTENANCE

Maintaining potted topiaries requires careful attention, the right environment, and consistent care. Let's explore some practical tips to help you keep your potted topiaries healthy and well maintained.

LIGHTING

Most topiaries thrive in bright light, needing at least six to eight hours of sunlight daily. As with any container plants (discussed in chapter 2) be sure to rotate your topiary at least once a month. This allows all sides of the plant to receive an equal amount of sunlight, resulting in more even growth. It also looks healthier and more attractive from every angle.

WATERING

Be sure to pot your topiaries in well-draining soil and keep the soil evenly moist. Lavender and angel vine have different watering needs. Lavender likes it drier. Water only when the top inch (2.5 cm) of soil feels dry. If it is hot or dry in your area, misting the foliage will help maintain humidity levels and prevent browning. Angel vine is more delicate and requires frequent watering; it will decline if allowed to dry out. Adding a layer of moist moss on top of your topiaries can also help slow down moisture loss. For this purpose, I prefer to use fresh sphagnum moss over peat moss.

FERTILIZING

Apply a slow-release, balanced fertilizer such as 10-10-10 or 20-20-20 every few weeks during the growing season, from early spring through early fall. Be sure to avoid overfeeding, which can damage the roots and foliage. During the winter, bring your topiaries indoors and reduce feeding to once a month.

FERTILIZER NUMBERS

Have you ever wondered what the numbers on a fertilizer package mean? In short, they represent the percentage of the essential plant macronutrients nitrogen, phosphorus, and potassium (N, P, K) within that fertilizer. These numbers are always listed in the same order: nitrogen, phosphorus, and potassium. Nitrogen promotes healthy, green leaves; phosphorus aids in root development and flower and fruit growth, and potassium helps plants stay healthy and resist disease, and it encourages fast growth.

↑ *A circular rosemary topiary paired with a string of pearls and vintage shears*

PRUNING

Always begin with a cleaned and sharpened pair of shears. Regular pruning is essential to maintain the desired shape of your topiaries as they grow. Prune lightly and often to maintain their current, tidy shape. Be conservative when pruning—you can always trim more, but you can't put it back! I always step back throughout the process to evaluate the shape and decide where next to trim, if at all. Also, be sure to leave a bit of new growth and do not prune into the old growth. I suggest pruning several times a year to maintain each plant's shape. Afterward, give the plant a thorough watering and be sure to keep it out of direct sunlight.

PEST CONTROL

Regularly inspect your topiaries for signs of trouble and treat any issues promptly with the appropriate natural or chemical solutions. Be on the lookout for aphids, thrips, scale, and spider mites, which cause significant damage if not dealt with promptly. If opting for organic solutions for pest control, insecticidal soaps are effective. Chemical options, such as insect, disease, and mite control, are also another solution. You can find three-in-one products, as well as organic alternatives, at most nurseries or hardware stores.

Using Garden Vegetables for Entertaining

Fresh produce from your vegetable garden can also be transformed into creative living décor. Here are some of my favorite ways to bring fruits and vegetables into the mix:

↑ Our Christmas tree is adorned with more dried orange garland from our orchard. I used only a handful of simple decorations as I wanted to replicate an old world style.

CENTERPIECES USING FRUITS AND VEGETABLES

Use your garden harvest with the floral design tips below to design and create stunning displays for your table. I like to put seasonal fruits and vegetables in the base of clear containers. I put a smaller container inside a larger one. In the gap between them, I place seasonal fruits, cranberries during winter or lemon slices in the summer, for a splash of color and to celebrate in-season fruits.

PRESERVING YOUR GARDEN HARVEST

Try these techniques for drying flowers, herbs, and fruits for use in cooking, arrangements, and décor:

1. **Air dried:** Simply bundle herbs or flowers together with twine and hang upside down in a cool, dry room.
2. **Oven dried:** Preheat your oven to 150°F (65°C) and insert a tray of herbs, leaving the door slightly ajar. Toss herbs every few minutes and bake until they turn crispy. Perfect for cooking.
3. **Dehydrated:** Place clean dry herbs or fruit slices in a dehydrator on a low setting. Dry until leaves easily crumble or fruit slices are no longer pliable.

The images on these pages show how I used dehydrated oranges and farm-sourced greenery and branches to beautifully decorate our mantel and Christmas tree for the holiday season.

← *Our Christmas mantel features a charming garland of dehydrated oranges paired with branches, greenery, and red holly berries, all sourced directly from the farm. I kept the décor simple, using only organic materials.*

→ *The tree also features red striped shoestring bows, vintage-style Santa ornaments, and pairs of taper candles.*

Using Your Harvests as Outdoor Décor

Using your garden harvests as outdoor décor is a beautiful way to bring the vibrant essence of your garden to the al fresco table and other outdoor spaces. By placing plants, herbs, flowers, and vegetables into your table settings and garden décor, you can create a unique, nature-inspired ambiance that celebrates each season's bounty.

The following are a few creative and practical ways to achieve this.

↑ Placing the finishing touches on my spring tablescape using hydrangeas and lemons

HERB TOPIARIES

You simply cannot go wrong with topiaries made from your favorite herbs and plants. Of course, selecting the right plants for the purpose is one of the major steps in creation. Some of my favorite plants for herbal topiaries are rosemary because of its classic scent and hardy growth; euonymus because of its dense, shiny foliage; myrtle with its elegant, evergreen appeal; and lavender with its display of subtle fragrance and delicate flowers.

I often decorate my herbal topiaries with vintage and hand-dyed silk ribbons for a timeless look. Rich greenery and the subtle sheen of silk provide a good balance and catch the eye to further beautify any setting. Herb topiaries can be arranged on mantels, as centerpieces, or can grace the length of a windowsill. They bring form and function to your décor, offering up a touch of nature and fragrance in carefully curated form.

GARDEN-THEMED ENTERTAINING SPACES

I love using seasonal flowers and fruits in my designs, especially in tablescapes, though they can be used anywhere or given as thoughtful gifts. To create the most impact in floral arrangements, cluster similar flowers together. For larger containers, I often use a variety of flowers and greenery, adding fruits at the base for added interest. For smaller arrangements, try using containers like votives with a single flower and leaf or shallow saucers to float a few of the same flowers such as roses, peonies, or gardenias with a touch of greenery. Try placing several of these along the center of a table to create a simple yet stunning visual effect, perfect for a garden party or bridal luncheon.

My lovely collection of assorted topiaries, some embellished with hand-dyed silk ribbons

REPURPOSING VINTAGE ITEMS

For unique containers, repurpose typical household items into garden treasures! You can also turn vintage household items into planters. I have used many unusual items as planters. My favorite find is a vintage wringer washing machine in the corner of my garden. I planted succulents in it and it creates the most interesting and unusual design element.

CRAFTING WITH GARDEN GOODS

You can use your garden goods for much more than culinary purposes. Beyond using fresh herbs to cook and can with fruits and vegetables, you can use your garden's bounty for crafting, too! Other uses include creating infused oils from herbs, making natural dyes from plants, pressing flowers, and even creating living

↑ *Various succulents planted in a repurposed vintage wringer washing machine*

wreaths. Let's look at two simple ways to craft with your garden goods, including how to create a living wreath and how to make DIY candles using pressed flowers and botanicals.

A DREAMY DIY: CRAFTING A LIVING WREATH

My all-time favorite piece of planted décor is my living wreath. It's truly an eye-catching DIY project! Not only is it beautiful in my space, but it is also functional. My daughter made one alongside me, and it was a great afternoon activity that we both enjoyed. One of the most exciting parts of this project was seeing how each of us customized our wreaths to fit our individual needs and likes. While my wreath was filled with herbs, my daughter's was packed with florals and decorative plants. If you are aiming for a wreath whose exclusive purpose is to be visually pleasing, flowering plants are a great option. If you are aiming for a wreath that is both beautiful and functional, using herbs is ideal. I keep my living wreath on the door just outside my kitchen so I can use the herbs whenever I wish. I simply clip some herbs off and add it right to the dish I'm cooking. Not only is this extremely convenient, cutting the herbs right off the wreath is beneficial to the plants themselves. Harvesting these herbs is essentially the same thing as pruning them, which promotes new and more prolific growth.

A living wreath is not only a unique piece of décor but also a testament to your gardening skills and love for nature. Let's explore how you can craft this lovely statement piece.

→ *My living wreath is planted with vinca, zinnias, ivy, thyme, oregano, dichondra, creeping Jenny, and an assortment of other greenery.*

How to Craft a Living Wreath

MATERIALS NEEDED:

- Two-part wire wreath form
- Jute liner
- Scissors
- Potting soil
- A collection of various 4-inch (10 cm) plants

WHERE CAN I FIND A WIRE WREATH FORM?

I buy my preferred wreath form from online retailers. Simply search for "living wreath form." The clip-together design makes it easy and quick to create your living wreaths. You can use them to decorate doors, walls, fences or tabletops. A variety of small annuals, herbs, or succulents makes for a striking presentation and unique garden decoration. A jute liner is often included with the wire wreath frame but buy one if not. The simple design of these living wreath rings allows you to plant wreaths for every season.

Pro Tip

Thoroughly moisten the liner before placing it inside the form. This step not only makes the liner easier to handle but gets the water right to the plants, giving them a head start in their new environment.

STEP 1:

Separate the two pieces of a two-part wire wreath form. Place the jute liner (plastic side in) and fill it with moistened potting soil. Then, cover the soil with the second jute piece and clip the wire frame into place. If done properly, you'll be able to plant on either side of the wreath.

STEP 2:

Using sharp scissors, cut X-shaped slits in the liner where you want to plant, keeping them evenly spaced for symmetry. It is worth your time to balance the look by mirroring your placement of plants on each side to maintain symmetry in the design.

STEP 3:

Gently guide the root mass of each plant through a slit, making sure the roots are in a relaxed position in the soil below the liner. Be patient and take your time to avoid damaging the plants as you push them through the slits. Adjust and firm the soil around the base of each plant for stability and to encourage healthy growth.

STEP 4:

After planting, place the wreath on its unplanted back for support. Then, water the wreath, making sure to soak the soil and the roots. Initial deep watering will help the plants establish. Leave the wreath in this horizontal position for a few days while the plants take the time to settle in. This resting period gets the plants to set roots into the soil to sustain them when the wreath is displayed in a vertical position.

Once the plants have had some time to settle in, you're ready to hang the wreath. Find a location where light and temperature meet the needs of your plants.

HOW DO I MAINTAIN MY LIVING WREATH?

- **Light:** Depending on your plants, part shade to full sun will mostly likely be best for annuals. Herbs and most succulents prefer as much sunlight as they can get. Be sure to read the garden tags inserted into newly purchased plants for the exact information on each plant.

- **Watering:** For light watering, you can use a gentle hose sprayer. Every so often, lay the wreath flat on the ground, water thoroughly and allow it to drain for twenty minutes before hanging it back up again.

- **Pinching back:** Vigorous growers need trimming every week or so. Continue to pinch the plants back to keep them bushy and preserve the wreath's round shape.

I Don't Have Jute Liners. Are There Any Other Options for Liners?

Liner material needs to be soft enough for you to make a hole and plant. At the same time, they need to be thick enough to hold the potting mix in place. If your frame does not include a liner, other options include Oregon green moss or coco fiber moss. You can buy both from online retailers.

← My newly planted living wreath on the greenhouse door

Making Your Own Botanical Candles

Making your own botanical candles is another delightful DIY garden project that adds a touch of nature. These handmade candles are not only a charming addition to any setting, a luncheon, special event, or cozy night in, but they bring the outdoors in. The result is a glowing, aromatic piece that exudes warmth and natural elegance. Here's a step-by-step guide on how to craft your own botanical candles.

MATERIALS NEEDED:

- Pressed flowers
- Pillar candles
- Wax paper
- Painter's tape
- Hair dryer

STEP 1:
Lay a strip of wax paper on a table and arrange pressed flowers on top.

STEP 2:
Gently roll the wax paper with flowers in place around the candle.

STEP 3:
Secure the wax paper around the candle with painter's tape.

STEP 4:
Use a hair dryer on its hottest setting to melt the wax so the flowers stick to the candle. Gently press the flowers into the warm wax every so often as you heat.

STEP 5:
Slowly unroll the wax paper and remove from the candle to reveal the perfect dried floral pillar!

↑ *My DIY botanical candle featured on my garden-inspired tablescape*

CREATE YOUR VISION GALLERY

Inspiration from my garden you can use
for creating your own living décor using
plants, flowers, and vegetables from
your garden.

→ *Snippers, twine, vintage
scoops, and gloves*

↑ *Blue hydrangeas with lemons in a farm fresh vase*

↑ *A favorite spring tablescape*

← *Indoor farm table with bittersweet berries*

Vintage Décor

Adding vintage articles and artifacts to your garden

Before we dive into decorating your space, let's focus on the importance of using vintage items in your home and garden. Vintage finds are unique, unlike mass-produced items. These finds are perfect to add to your space, as they stand out. Not only do they provide an aesthetically pleasing feel to your space, but they also tell a story based on their past. Some of my favorite vintage finds are the ones that hold history within themselves. One example is my *cazo de cobre* pot, which I found at the Round Top Antiques Fair in Round Top, Texas. This hand-hammered copper pot was once used in cooking in Central Mexico. Its patina is the most beautiful turquoise color! Because the pot itself was more than four feet (1.2 m) in diameter, I made it into a table. A local woodworker customized a tabletop and a base to fit the pot. The table is now both beautiful and functional piece. I beautify it with seasonal centerpieces and serve food and drinks on it.

The Versatility of Vintage

A common theme throughout my space is transformed vintage objects. Often, I find unique pieces, and then I transform them into usable pieces. I bought a white 1940s wringer washing machine and put Boston ferns in it. It is rusting under our oak tree, gaining character and patina by the day. My second washer, a mint green color, still works! I put various succulents in it and transformed it into a potting container. Vintage pieces always offer versatility. It just takes the right eye to bring it out!

↑ *Summertime capture of my collection of vintage seed boxes atop our cazo de cobre pot in the silo*

→ *Here is another view of my seed boxes adorned for Christmas, alongside my collection of vintage sheep and lamb figurines.*

↑ *My vintage seed cabinet houses my collection of antique tools and pots.*

Curating Your Collection

While beginning your curating journey may seem daunting, the hardest part is just taking the first step. It is an incredibly rewarding hobby that is well worth your efforts. Over time, your collection will continue to grow, and before you know it, you will be giving curating advice to others. When searching for vintage items, start at a vintage or antique shop or fair. When I was beginning my journey, I searched the Internet for "where to purchase vintage goods in my area." This is how I found the Round Top Antiques Fair. I listed the items I wanted and stuck to looking for those. I perused a variety of booths and found some gems. I didn't find everything on my list, but a big part of this hobby is the thrill of the hunt!

↑ *My darling collection of mini pots displayed in a small birdbath*

Your Vintage Space

How to use your vintage finds depends on what they are. Tables and chairs make great focal points of your space. If you have smaller vintage items, use them as decorative pieces. I like to think of these as unique treasures in your space.

Decorating with smaller decorative pieces can be such a fun, creative way to add personality and whimsy to your space. One of my favorite strategies for decorating with smaller pieces is grouping similar objects to create collections. For instance, several topiaries make a striking statement displayed on a table. Similarly, grouping a collection of vintage white Santa mugs on a tray or in a cabinet creates a curated look that feels intentional and visually appealing.

Another good tip is to group items of the same material for a polished display, e.g., all wooden or all metal photo frames, glass vases, ceramic pots, or woven baskets. This continuity keeps an arrangement from looking cluttered. By grouping like materials and colors, you showcase the individual textures and tones of the pieces while keeping an aesthetic balance.

The key to decorating with smaller treasures is to give them a chance to shine. When you group similar items, they create a bigger visual impact than when they're scattered around a room. Grouping draws attention to the details and craftsmanship of your pieces. Whether you're arranging topiaries, vintage collectibles, or matching frames, intentional groupings can turn even the smallest decorative items into meaningful and eye-catching focal points in your home.

One larger "treasure" we acquired was an antique silo! Built in the 1890s, our silo came from another farm. We disassembled and transported it from Mt. Sterling, Illinois, to southeast Texas.

↑ *An assortment of different succulents arranged in a vintage 1940s wringer washing machine*

Once it arrived, we reassembled it on a concrete pad. Every part of it is original, including the dovetail-jointed posts. Although I have all the original panels to enclose the silo, I leave them off for air flow and aesthetics. I also created a unique "chandelier" inside using found goods. I found a vintage hog feed ring at the Round Top Antiques Fair and asked my electrician to bring

↑ *Our copper* cazo de cobre *pot table is adorned for the Fourth of July festivities in the silo.*

my vision to reality. I wanted to use it as a chandelier, and he made that happen. He used metal pipe fittings with hanging lights inside for a cascading effect. He hung it in the middle of the silo and secured it from either side with metal chains so the wind could not take it. The chandelier gives the silo the most beautiful ambiance! Aside from the photo on the next page, you'll hear more about this unique light and see more photos of it in chapter 7 where I discuss lighting. The silo is also where the earlier referenced vintage *cazo de cobre* copper pot table is used, too.

Our vintage hog feeder chandelier

CREATE YOUR VISION GALLERY

Here is some inspiration from my garden you can use to find creative ways to successfully include vintage articles and artifacts in your own garden.

↑ *Antique seed cabinet*

↑ *Vintage Christmas greens sign*

↑ *A collection of antique treasures on display*

↓ Vintage small seed box

↑ Vintage greenhouse sign

*→ Close-up of the seed
cabinet artwork*

A Porch to Ponder

Shaping your welcome space into more than the average entryway

No matter the season, the porch is always a favorite spot to sit, relax, and enjoy the fruits of your labor. A porch welcomes guests and creates the first impression of your home. Because the summer Texas climate is very humid and extremely hot, you can often find me here after a day in the garden. The porch is also a great place for family to gather. Everyone enjoys relaxing on the porch after completing a long day's work, whether it be finishing horses, harvesting crops, fertilizing the fields, or feeding our cattle.

Our porch offers us a space to cool off and socialize with one another, while still spending some valuable time outside. Because Texas winters are moderate, we use the porch most days of the year. I enjoy decorating it for each season. In cooler weather, you will often find cozy blankets and vintage pillows on the bed swing and rockers.

The Right Impression

Your porch makes a first impression on visitors and creates an inviting atmosphere. It also develops a lasting impression and impact on your guests. For this reason, I adopted the concept of "simple yet effective," and have kept this motto at the forefront, even to this day. Here are some easy ways to make your porch a more welcoming space:

- Adorn the entry. Whether it be with blooming trees, topiaries, ferns, ornamental potted plants, or wreaths, greenery always enhances the aesthetic of your porch. For a symmetrical look, flank your door with bedding containers or pots.

- If space allows, offer a place for guests to relax and sit awhile. Use rockers or gliders with cozy throws and pillows for a relaxed feel.

- Set out a large welcome mat. Not only will it protect your floor and be available to clean your shoes off, but it will also serve as an extension of your indoor living space.

- Build a gently curved walkway to your door. Curves offer a more casual and natural feel than straight lines. You can use a variety of materials other than concrete for a more interesting look. Try steppingstones, concrete pavers, or flagstones.

- Add containers. I like simple containers in creamy white colors or seagrass material. These bring a vertical aspect to your porch and tie everything together. If you like color, consider using a combination of planter boxes or bright pots in different shapes and sizes for more interest, then fill them with vibrant flowers. If you have steps, try placing the pot nearest to the door at a higher level and add a few more pots cascading down the steps. I prefer symmetry, so I replicate the arrangement on both sides for a balanced look.

- Lanterns of various sizes with either fairy lights or outdoor battery-powered flameless candles add an extra well-lit touch at night. For porch ceiling lighting, think beyond metal. If your house paint color is neutral, try brightly painted gooseneck lights on either side of the door for a pop of color. Rattan pendants can be a great option, too, for a covered porch, adding a more relaxed feel.

↑ *Our spring bed swing is adorned with beautiful soft floral pillows and a vintage quilt.*

↑ *An antique chest acts as a side table next to the bed swing, holding a mix of vintage and new gardening books along with spring planters.*

↑ *A small vintage French table is used as an additional table on the porch.*

- Paint your porch flooring and steps to match the color of your home's siding for a seamless appearance. This is one of the most economical ways to transform any porch. Enhance the space with outdoor furniture and planters (as mentioned previously) to create an enticing and inviting environment for your guests. If your siding is a neutral color, consider painting your door in a bold color to make it stand out. Accent your porch décor with matching accessories, such as pots, pillows, and flowers, in the same color for a cohesive look.

- Sprinkle in vintage finds. Your favorite vintage finds personalize your porch décor and give it a style unique to you. On our porch, you will find a vintage chest, a small French table, and several chippy white smaller tables around the rockers. Not only do I use these to display colorful plants and small candles, but on a hot summer's day, I rest a cold glass of iced tea on them. On a cold winter's night, you can find a warm cup of cocoa there.

Our summer porch corner features a cozy rocker and a vintage wicker general post office cart from England, filled with Kimberly Queen ferns.

↑ *Christmas rockers on the porch with both new and vintage cozy throws, perfect to curl up with on chilly nights*

The Versatility of Color Schemes

Let's visit the design principle of color schemes a bit more, particularly as they pertain to welcoming porch décor. As you learned in the garden design chapter, *monochromatic* color schemes focus on one color and its various shades, tints, and tones. Pair porch décor with varying hues of one color to create a cohesive and harmonious look. When different hues of the same color are combined, the result is a polished and eye-catching appearance.

On the other hand, *color blocking* involves pairing opposite colors on the color wheel (known as *complementary colors* in color theory). This technique creates a vibrant, eye-catching contrast that brings a striking appearance to

your porch (or any other space for that matter). Pick bold combinations, such as blue and orange, red and green, or purple and yellow. These pairings make a strong statement and are ideal for porches that aim to be bright and impactful. Once you have chosen your primary color scheme, you can then follow up with secondary or tertiary colors in your design if you so choose.

Christmas bed swing decorated with both handmade and vintage pillows

A Joy for All Seasons

Decorating the porch space is always a joy for me. In a recent year, I created a stunning fall-themed archway piece above the front door using a large fallen branch, adorned with fall décor and finished with twinkle lights; my favorite porch creation to date! I completed the look with colorful mums and cornstalks. I also attached cornstalks to the silo and greenhouse entries and to each column on the porch, to unify the design. I like to place bundles of cornstalks in bushel baskets filled with hay and smaller pumpkins to anchor them.

↑ *A cozy spot to relax on our bed swing decorated for fall*

→ *Our fall porch features my homemade decorative archway above the door, crafted with old tree branches from the farm as the base for the décor.*

CREATE YOUR VISION GALLERY

Inspiration from my garden you can use for shaping your porch into more than the average entryway.

↑ Christmas bed swing with handmade Santa pillows

↑ Spring porch with rockers

→ Fall porch décor

← Christmas daytime porch with cozy pillows and blankets— both vintage and new

↓ Seasonal doormats add an extra sweet touch.

↑ Fall daytime porch with steps

A Well-Lit Space

Creating a warmly lit outdoor space to enhance the ambiance and mood

D on't underestimate the critical role of lighting in setting the mood. No matter how much effort you put into perfecting your outdoor space, lighting can be the deciding factor in its success! Lighting allows you to emphasize the areas you want to showcase while diverting attention from those you'd rather keep in the background. Without proper lighting, all your meticulously planned décor can easily go unnoticed.

Lighting in a garden or outdoor space can come from a variety of sources, each offering their own unique purpose and charm. There are many options available, which include electric light fixtures, walkway lights, strung party lights or bistro lighting, candles, fire pits, lanterns, and more. With outdoor lighting, choose options that reflect the style and theme of your garden but also address other concerns, such as safety. Proper lighting improves visibility and can prevent accidents, especially around pathways, steps, and uneven surfaces.

You can buy solar versions of many lights, like walkway lights and string lights. They are budget-friendly since they eliminate the need for extensive wiring. Solar lights do have some drawbacks, though, such as reduced brightness or effectiveness on cloudy days.

In choosing lighting, consider whether you are looking for temporary or permanent fixtures. Temporary lighting includes easy-to-move-around fixtures, like string lights and portable lanterns, great for seasonal decorations or certain special events. Long term, such options do not hold up as well and require higher maintenance. Permanent fixtures, such as installed pathway lights or electric fixtures, are more durable, ensuring that your solution is long-lasting. However, they may have higher upfront costs and a more complex installation processes.

The balance between style and practicality is what makes an outdoor space appealing and well lit. The perfect lighting plan enhances the beauty of your garden while also ensuring your space is functional and safe.

The silo and table are beautifully lit for an evening Christmas celebration.

Outdoor Spaces with Bistro and Gooseneck Lighting

For larger areas, such as my vegetable garden, I use bistro lighting overhead. I hang many strands around the garden, in oak trees, and above the farmhouse table and walkway to the silo. Gooseneck lighting is above all entries to the tool shed and greenhouse. Dutch doors flank each building. The greenhouse has functional lighting for working inside at night, and a small chandelier, on a dimmer switch, for a cozier feel at night.

↑ *The greenhouse, farmhouse table, and silo are warmly illuminated on a crisp fall evening.*

Vintage Chandelier Drops for a Touch of Reflective Light

For some time now, I have been collecting crystal chandelier drops. I visit antique fairs and vintage stores, and I even made a recent visit to a street fair in New York City's Chelsea Market, where I found an overabundance of them. After I amassed a generous amount, I used floral wire to attach them to the branches of our old oak tree, which hovers over the farmhouse table. The chandelier drops gently swing in the breeze of the night and cast a beautiful prismatic effect over the table. It's the perfect finishing touch, like icing on the cake!

↑ *Vintage chandelier drops dangle from the oak tree, swaying gently in the breeze and casting the most enchanting light.*

Pro Tip

Use the same paint color and lighting concept on all outdoor building structures to create a cohesive look throughout your outdoor space. Use clear lighting at night in the garden and bistro lights to create a warm ambiance.

← *A detailed view of our greenhouse ceiling chandelier adorned with Christmas boughs and pepper berries for the holiday season*

Using Light to Create a Magical Atmosphere

During the holiday season, we install cascading lights above each open panel around the silo. It creates the most beautiful and magical atmosphere! Above each open panel, we installed gooseneck lighting to match the lighting on the greenhouse and toolshed. Inside the silo is one of my all-time favorite repurposed vintage pieces, the chandelier made from a vintage hog feeder ring that I discussed in an earlier chapter (see page 122).

The farmhouse table is always a quaint spot for a lovely dinner on any given night. Candlelight always elevates the mood and atmosphere. Candles in various sizes, including votives (for intimate lighting), tapers (for ambient lighting), and pillars (for more substantial lighting), are a must. Although wax candles always create the perfect glow, I opt for battery-operated votives and tapers that flicker. They maintain their shape and are a bit safer, especially in outside elements like wind. I have a beautiful wooden centerpiece with hanging bottles and a long tray. I use fairy lights all around this piece to create the most wonderful nighttime centerpiece.

We recently hung two beautifully repurposed chandeliers over the farmhouse table (see photo on page 147). I had a pair of forged brass chandeliers with a shiny, polished finish. But the bright metal didn't match the rustic charm of our farmhouse aesthetic. We gave them new life by painting them a matte black, which instantly gave them a more understated and timeless look. I love the creativity that comes with repurposing items. It's so rewarding to transform something unexpected into a piece that truly feels at home in our space.

↑ *The chandelier in the silo, adorned for the Fourth of July*

To add more visual interest, we hung the chandeliers at varying heights, allowing them to stand out individually while creating a harmonious look together. Paired with delicate crystal drops and surrounded by the warm glow of bistro lights, they bring a perfect ambiance to the farmhouse table, making it a cozy, intimate spot to gather.

↑ *These repurposed chandeliers were recently installed above the farmhouse table, providing excellent ambient lighting.*

One Christmas, I also showcased our interior dining room chandeliers. Our custom twelve-foot farmhouse table fits its space perfectly and accommodates our large family gatherings. I knew I wanted to feature our newly installed dimmable farmhouse chandeliers, which were once fans. While in NYC for the 2024 Better Homes and Gardens Stylemaker event, I spent hours at an incredible vintage ribbon shop browsing unique ribbons for the chandeliers. I picked out red and green plaids for the holiday season.

Back home in Texas, I adorned the chandelier arms with fresh pepper berries, seeded eucalyptus, and tiny lights, then tied simple shoelace bows with my vintage ribbons, letting them hang down elegantly. A vintage-style concrete Christmas goose serves as the centerpiece, complete with a simple bow around its neck (see photo on page 150). Inspired by my chandeliers, this has become my favorite tablescape to date!

Our outdoor entertaining area beneath the old oak tree, beautifully decorated for Christmas guests

Christmas chandeliers adorned with pepper berries, greenery, and vintage ribbons

↑ *Clusters of votive candles provide warm, intimate lighting for our Christmas table.*

To add nighttime ambience outdoors, I also like to place lanterns filled with small string lights and battery-powered pillars around the garden. I like to emulate warmth and create a cozy atmosphere with these lanterns. That is the beauty of using battery-powered elements: They are convenient for illuminating without necessarily needing outlets or having the risks of real flames. These lanterns lend a soft, magical light to any outdoor space, from the patio to the porches, garden paths, and even the dining areas. The flickers from the battery-operated candles and the delicate twinkling of the string lights are the perfect layering to create an enchanted effect and a sense of special coziness and charm.

You can buy lanterns in a variety of finishes and styles, from rustic metal to antique bronze or sleek black. Choose lanterns based on your style preference and place them strategically: on tables, steps, or even hanging from hooks, to add depth and dimension, making sure every corner is bathed in ambient light. Complete the look by placing the lanterns near either potted plants or floral arrangements, extending the glow and balancing the light to create an illuminated garden experience ideal for nights of relaxation or times of entertaining.

Pro Tip

Group votives of like materials together for more visual impact, rather than scattering them individually across an area.

Antique lanterns are a classic and timeless option for outdoor porch lighting, too, bringing charm and beauty to enhance the transitional spaces between the home and garden. Copper and zinc can develop a weathered patina that adds vintage appeal to any space. Whether placed on either side of a doorway or suspended overhead, vintage-inspired lanterns elevate the evening curb appeal of any home, garden, or outdoor space.

← *Two sizes of lanterns filled with fairy lights rest at the entry of the silo.*

WELL-LIT VINTAGE FINDS

Get creative with lighting your vintage finds! So many items can be repurposed into lights. I punched holes in a vintage minnow bucket and filled it with fairy lights, as well as a mason jar. The minnow bucket glows stunningly through the holes.

→ *A touch of ambient light crafted from fairy lights in a minnow bucket and a mason jar*

Playing with Fire

Few elements create as much warmth and atmosphere as an outdoor fire. There's an undeniable charm in watching the glowing flames that captivates the senses and invites relaxation. Whether fueled by gas, propane, or traditional wood, outdoor fire pits seamlessly enrich any space by offering a comfortable ambiance. These features provide the perfect backdrop for gatherings, allowing friends and family to share stories, enjoy the crisp air, and create lasting memories throughout the seasons. The addition of an outdoor fire pit is not just practical, it adds a touch of timeless comfort to any outdoor setting.

↑ *Our inviting outdoor space and fire pit nestled beneath the old oak tree*

↑ *Our firepit is used year-round. The area is also lit with bistro lights, candles, and string lights.*

Maximize Your Space for Lighting—Go Vertical!

Take advantage of every opportunity to experiment with outdoor lighting. Even your trees can become beautiful focal points! Quite possibly the most impactful way we've enhanced our outdoor space is by adding decorative lighting to the oldest oak tree on the farm. We hung nine illuminated grapevine balls in the branches for some natural elegance with a bit of whimsy.

Each grapevine ball was suspended at a different height to give the display depth and interest. These handmade spheres range in diameter from an impressive thirty inches (76 cm) down to a more modest twenty-four inch (61 cm), twenty inch (51 cm), and eighteen inch (46 cm). This variation adds a dynamic, layered effect that captivates both day and night. We were lucky to have a power source near this tree, which made the project much more manageable.

We took it to the next level and made it magical at sunset by wrapping miniature lights

with a brown cord around each grapevine ball. The brown cord was a well thought out detail so it would not contrast with the grapevine structure, letting the lights glow freely. And to make it even better, the captivating warm light appears to float in the tree, casting soft light over the landscape with a sense of wonder.

It turns the oak tree into a focal point that is not only beautiful but also serves to illuminate the space when we're hosting outdoor gatherings, dinners, or just spending quiet moments outside. The soft glow of the lighted grapevine balls invites you to a place where you can entertain guests or enjoy quiet moments under the stars. Adding lighting into unexpected places, including up in the trees, expands the garden's dimension and warmth, and helps to create an intimate outdoor space.

Grapevine balls, in various sizes, cast a beautiful glow beneath our towering oak tree.

The Value of Lighting

Lighting is one of the most important design elements for safely enjoying your garden both day and night. It also lets you be creative and turns your outdoor space into a warmly lit haven. The right lighting can turn any given setting from drab to cozy and warm or even to dramatically striking. Whether you plan to entertain friends, have dinner al fresco, or want to spend an evening under a star-studded sky, a well-conceived lighting design serves to enhance the experience and enjoyment of your outdoors.

↑ *A winter view just outside the silo, illuminated with cascading string lights, a chandelier, and gooseneck lights above the entrance*

→ *Christmas porch at night illuminated with canned lights and string lights*

Our farmhouse table and silo adorned with fall décor and cascading lights

CREATE YOUR VISION GALLERY

Inspiration from my garden you can use to create a warmly lit outdoor space of your own.

→ *Votive candles are easy ways to add a touch of light to your tablescape no matter the season.*

↓ *Different lighting sources can combine together for a beautiful effect.*

↑ *Inside the silo with chandelier and Christmas trees*

↑ *Bistro lighting in the garden is both practical and attractive.*

← *Our up-lit water fountain at dusk*

↑ *The winter garden with bistro lighting*

Friends Among the Flowers

How to Incorporate Pollinator-Friendly Plants into the Farmhouse Garden

Did you know such pollinators as bees, butterflies, and hummingbirds are responsible for many of the foods, beverages, and medicines we use daily? For this reason, as well as the declining populations of many pollinators, it's time for us to make a positive impact and create an ecosystem pollinators can rely on, no matter how large or small our gardens may be.

Native plants are the best option for supporting pollinators. Both native plants and their pollinators have evolved together to fit your specific climate and growing conditions. Planting a pollinator-friendly garden not only adds beauty to your landscape, but it is an environmentally conscious effort, too. Such a design provides nectar, pollen, and a safe habitat for supporting the pollinator population. Your county agricultural extension service can provide relevant resources on how to create a pollinator-friendly habitat and which native plants to include, as well as many other informative solutions and needs specific to your locality.

Another way to support pollinators is to add a water source to your garden. As discussed on previous pages, I have a petrified stone disappearing fountain directly in the middle of the vegetable garden. It provides an easy-to-access source of water for pollinators. A water source like a fountain, small pond, or container water garden is a fantastic way to elevate your garden space and encourage the presence of pollinators (you'll find more about providing water to pollinators on page 170). These little friends are essential to a thriving garden—I would be nowhere without them! In addition to lots of vegetables, I've also begun incorporating many flowers into my vegetable garden to attract and support a diversity of pollinators. Not only are these sweet creatures crucial to our environment, but they are beautiful to watch, too!

Pollinators and Their Importance Within Ecosystems

Pollinators transfer pollen from flower to flower as they feed on their nectar, a crucial role for the fertilization of many plants. There are a wide range of pollinator types, including bees, hummingbirds, butterflies, moths, beetles, flies, and wasps. Pollinators are essential to the process of ensuring genetic diversity in plants. These little guys play a massive role in the health of ecosystems worldwide, including your garden!

↑ Including pollinator plants, like these garlic chives, in your garden is both helpful and beautiful.

YOUR GARDEN IS THRIVING THANKS TO SYMBIOSIS

Plants provide food and habitat for all sorts of wildlife: insects, birds, small mammals, lizards, frogs, toads, and so many more. The symbiotic relationship among all these creatures and plants provides nature (and, therefore, the garden) with all the tools necessary for its survival, as it creates a balanced and thriving ecosystem. The role of pollinators is particularly valuable to food gardeners because when there is effective pollination, fruit and vegetable plants produce a higher yield. In other words, when pollinators are happy because they have an ample food source and shelter, the food plants are also happy and can produce more. To me, this is part of the beauty of gardening, witnessing the wonders of this symbiotic relationship. It is a part of the garden that you need to take the time to appreciate!

POLLINATORS AS INDICATOR SPECIES

Pollinators sometimes act as indicator species. This means their presence—and the quantity and quality of it—reflects the health of the overall ecosystem. When indicator pollinator species decline, it leads to devastating effects on the overall ecosystem where they live. Because there is nothing facilitating the reproductive cycle of certain plants, those plant species decline. This leads to a decrease in food, resources, and shelter for other wildlife in the area. Without pollinators, a balanced ecosystem would be impossible.

Outside of the home garden, pollinators are responsible for the success of many fruits, vegetables, and nuts that make their way to our tables. It is with their help that our economic system *is* a system. Pollinators play a crucial role in the production of hundreds of crops around the world.

In summary, pollinators are fundamental to the health and proper functioning of farm and garden ecosystems, as well as wild ecosystems across the globe. The next time you smell a beautiful jasmine or spot a bright marigold, thank your local pollinators for helping it grow!

Let's learn more about the problems pollinators are facing and how gardeners can help.

Pro Tip

Remove faded or spent flowers regularly to promote continuous blooming throughout the season.

ZINNIA LOVE

Zinnias are some of the most colorful and long-blooming seasonal flowers. Here are the top five reasons I use them in the garden:

1. Zinnias have long-lasting seasonal color. They are very good about reblooming, so you are guaranteed to have a rainbow of colors all through the season.
2. They are incredibly low maintenance. Zinnias are easy growers and do not require a lot of care. The only maintenance that is needed is the occasional deadheading, which encourages reblooming. Cut the stem off below the faded bloom just above the next set of healthy leaves.
3. Zinnias are incredibly heat- and drought-tolerant. This is particularly beneficial for my garden since we frequently face heat spells and droughts in Texas.
4. Zinnias are inexpensive to plant and maintain. A packet of seeds is all you need for season-long color.
5. Pollinators are especially attracted to bright and colorful zinnias.

A Beautiful Garden DIY:
Building a Trumpet Honeysuckle
Gateway Arch to Attract Hummingbirds

↑ *A DIY cattle panel arch with a trumpet honey-suckle vine. Look closely to spot our beautiful American Paint Horse, Fancy, in the back-ground.*

Are you searching for a simple, easy, but at the same time, impressive method to get your garden ready for spring? Building a homemade garden gateway arch can reimagine the way your garden space looks, serving as an inviting entrance into your outdoor space and adding structure and visual interest. Not only does a gateway arch provide a beautiful focal point, but it is also a perfect support for climbing plants like roses or clematis, or hummingbird-friendly vines like honeysuckles, cypress vine, or morning glories. The plants can be grown at the arch's base and their branches woven into the arch to create a stunning natural display.

It doesn't have to be complicated or expensive to build a DIY garden gateway arch. You can design an arch that's suitable for your garden's style out of the most ordinary materials. Whether you prefer the rustic look of natural wood or the more polished appearance of painted metal, the options are endless.

First, decide where the arch is going to be placed, perhaps over a gate or path, or across an entrance to a bed to create a division between areas. Set it into the ground securely for optimum stability, making sure the structure can hold the weight of growing plants and several seasons of weather. Of course, once your arch is up, you can add some decoration to it, such as twinkling string lights in the evening or small hanging planters to add some additional greenery. I installed uplighting on my rose arch to give it the perfect evening glow.

Constructing a DIY Arch

With minimal effort, a homemade gateway arch can easily be the crowning jewel of your garden. Let me walk you through how I created my DIY trumpet honeysuckle vine arch in the garden.

MATERIALS NEEDED:

- 4 to 6 foot (1.2 to 2 m) metal T-posts
- 16 by 4 foot (1.2 by 5 m) cattle fence panel
- Zip ties
- Hammer

STEP 1:
Drive all four T-posts securely into the ground. These will frame both sides of the arch with one on each of the arch's four corners. Be sure to account for the width of your cattle panel for exact placement of the T-posts.

STEP 2:
Place one end of the cattle panel inside one of the pairs of posts. Then, gently bend the panel to create an arch so it rests inside the other pair of posts, mirroring the other side. You should be left with an upside-down letter U; this is the frame of your arch.

STEP 3:
Zip-tie the cattle panel to the T-posts in multiple spots to secure the arch in place.

STEP 4:
Plant your favorite climbing vine on either side and let the fun begin!

Not only is this a beautiful addition to your garden, but it also attracts lots of pollinators, too!

↑ *A hummingbird flutters around the trumpet honeysuckle vine arch in the summer.*

HUNGRY HUMMINGBIRD

Did you know hummingbirds can consume more than twice their body weight in one day!

The Pollinator Problem

Pollinator populations are in decline due to a multitude of factors including habitat loss, pesticide use, persistent takeover by invasive species, and insufficient conservation efforts. To start, the increase in urbanization and man-made infrastructure, along with the removal of natural spaces such as wildflower meadows, reduces the availability of resources pollinators need to thrive. This, in turn, decreases the biodiversity of the area. Additionally, while the use of pesticides can be beneficial in keeping harmful bug species at bay, these products also harm pollinators and may deter them from feeding on plants. So, while the "bad guys" are removed, unfortunately, so are the "good guys." The overuse of pesticides is harmful to overall pollinator populations.

Another major character that comes into play is the increasing prevalence of invasive introduced plant species. Invasive introduced plant species include those that are not native to an area and exhibit aggressive growth. These plants often hail from another continent entirely. These species can sometimes become aggressively competitive and take over areas that might otherwise be filled with the native flowering plants relied on by pollinators.

Sadly, another factor that is contributing to the decline of pollinator populations is the lack of conservation efforts by the public. The source of this is often a lack of awareness. Many people are unaware of this growing problem, and therefore, take no action to help preserve these important creatures.

The good news is, while some contributing factors are hard for us to control individually, awareness and education can be spread very easily! Just by reading this chapter and educating yourself, you are doing something to help sustain pollinators. Now, let us dive into some physical ways you can help promote the health of pollinators, including inviting them into your own garden.

HIDDEN IN PLAIN SIGHT

Did you know killdeer birds lay their eggs right on the ground, often among stones, cleverly hiding them in plain sight from predators?

→ *Killdeer bird on our farm guarding her nest with eggs*

Attracting Pollinators

To participate in pollinator-friendly gardening, you are going to design your garden in a way that attracts pollinators to it and gives them the resources they need to thrive. Start by selecting various plants that flower at different times throughout the growing season. Intentionally staggering bloom times ensures pollinators have a sufficient and consistent source of food within your garden. Also, make sure to select plants that are native to your area whenever possible; they are more likely to attract pollinators, as the two have evolved and adapted to your environment together!

Another way to attract pollinators is to dedicate a corner of your garden to them. In addition to flowering annuals and perennials, plant herbs, shrubs, and grasses that are thick and dense, providing habitat and shelter for pollinators year-round. These are great spots for pollinators to hide, overwinter, or even just rest for a while. Dense plants also provide protection for pollinators in the form of shelter from dangers such as strong winds and predators. Some examples of dense herbs that live in my garden include lavender and rosemary. Not only are they attractive to pollinators, but they also provide a soothing aroma in my space, which I love! In this corner of your garden, plant flowering plants that are attractive to both the bees and the butterflies seeking out their nectar. In addition, plant host plants for the caterpillars of the butterflies found in your area. My favorite butterfly is the monarch, so I plant milkweed because it is a host plant for monarch caterpillars (you'll read more about supporting the monarch in a later section of this chapter). I also plant fennel and parsley for the swallowtail butterfly caterpillars.

Pro Tip

Both European honey bees and North America's 3,500-plus native bee species are important pollinators, and if they are not provoked, most are actually very docile!

↑ *Swallowtail butterfly perched on a butterfly bush*

As mentioned earlier in the chapter, while providing pollinators with a source of food is essential, water should not be forgotten. Keep a shallow water source in your garden for pollinators to stop by and drink from. Just like it is for you or me, water is essential for pollinators to carry out their daily functions. It provides them with hydration, a means of cleansing, and a way to cool down on a hot day. Whether it be a birdbath, a pond, or a simple dish, water is essential for pollinators to thrive and to do their jobs. One of my favorite ways to keep water for my pollinators is in bee cups. These are cute little cups that hold just a teaspoon of water for my sweet pollinator friends!

In addition to water sources, place nesting sites for pollinators throughout your garden. One of my favorite nesting sites is a native bee hotel. These small additions to your garden are also aesthetically pleasing, as they are mainly made from wood, matching the natural landscape. Bee hotels are used by a few different small native bee species, such as orchard mason bees and leaf cutter bees, for the entirety of their lifetimes. If an egg is laid in the hotel, the larval bee that emerges from it stays housed in the structure until it is ready to emerge as a fully grown adult! Keep bee hotels clean and maintain them regularly to prevent the spread of disease.

PREFERRED COLORS

Different species of pollinators are attracted to specific colors. While many bee species are attracted to flowers with a cool tone, hummingbirds and butterflies are more heavily drawn to colors within a warm palette.

Filling my bee cups with water

POLLINATOR-FRIENDLY FLOWERS

Flowering plants not only enhance your landscape, but they also shelter and feed pollinators, too. Below is a list of some pollinator-favorite flowers and herbs to consider adding to your garden:

Asters	Gomphrena
Bee balm	Lavender
Celosia	Marigolds
Chrysanthemums	Milkweed
Cockscomb	Rudbeckia
Columbine	Sedum
Coneflower	Sunflowers
Dahlias	Yarrow
Geranium	Zinnias

Monarch butterfly resting on a Texas bluebonnet flower

One of America's Most Iconic Butterflies: The Monarch

Though many legends abound about how the monarch butterfly got its common name, people often say the monarch butterfly is the most beautiful butterfly, and so it became known as the "king of butterflies," or the "monarch."

Regardless of the true source of its common name, the monarch butterfly plays an important role in many of the ecosystems of the New World. It pollinates many types of flowers as it feeds on their nectar. Unfortunately, the monarch population is down significantly from record numbers just thirty years ago. Climate change, drought, the widespread use of herbicides, and a decrease in milkweed (its larval host plant) are other contributing factors. The latter is significant because this is the only species of plant a monarch caterpillar can eat.

Monarch butterflies are easily recognized by their bright orange wings with black stripes. Although males and females look similar, they are easy to tell apart. Males have a thicker black spot along one of the black stripes at the bottom of each wing, while females do not. Monarchs also have one of the longest and most amazing migration journeys in the animal kingdom. It reaches from Canada all the way down to the mountains of Mexico. We live in Texas and are fortunate to be right along their migration path. They start their northern journey and stop at feeding and breeding grounds to lay eggs. They then die, and a new generation continues the migration. Their entire annual journey may take over three generations to complete! Once they have completed their northern journey to Canada, the cycle repeats itself. There are two primary migration journeys for monarch butterflies; they travel north in spring and return south in fall.

On their migration route, monarchs stop at nectar corridors, which are familiar places to stop and refuel on nectar before continuing their journey. I love to foster their lifecycle and migration by planting plenty of milkweed in my garden. As previously mentioned, this is the only plant the tiny caterpillars (larvae) have evolved to eat. Without a milkweed source (the host plant) the larvae are not able to develop and pupate into adult butterflies. Milkweed also contains compounds that make it—and the monarchs that evolved to feed on it—poisonous to potential predators.

If you live in a warm growing zone like mine, be sure to plant only North American native species of milkweed, as South or Central American species bloom throughout the year and can potentially be harmful to monarchs. Why? It is because, when these tropical species of milkweed are available, monarchs may stop to feed and lay eggs too early on their route northward, thus hindering the migration process. It also makes the monarch more prone to pathogens and diseases that can also be detrimental to the monarch population and migration process.

TASTE AND SMELL

Did you know monarch butterflies taste with their feet and smell with their antennae, both processes that help them identify their host plants prior to egg laying?

WAYS YOU CAN HELP THE DECLINING MONARCH POPULATION

It's easy: Simply plant milkweed to support monarch larvae and provide nectar-bearing flowers for adult monarch butterflies. Any size garden, no matter how small, can make a difference in supporting monarchs as well as other pollinators, so I encourage you to try. Involve your children or grandchildren in the process of planting milkweed. It is such a fun way to get them interested and excited about gardening, too!

ALL IN A NAME

Milkweed is so named for its latex, a milky substance that exudes when the plant is damaged. It is not a weed at all but rather a beautiful wildflower that comes in a variety of colors.

BLUEBONNETS

Did you know the Texas bluebonnet, a hardy winter annual native to Texas, was named after the sunbonnets worn by pioneer women to protect themselves from the harsh sun?

↑ *A lovely shot of a bee on the vitex near the silo*

Beautiful summer coneflowers just outside the silo

CREATE YOUR VISION GALLERY

Inspiration from my garden you can use for incorporating pollinator-friendly plants and practices into your own farmhouse garden.

→ *Birdhouse with roses*

↑ *Salvia is an excellent pollinator plant for the garden.*

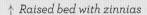

↑ *Raised bed with zinnias*

↑ *Swallowtail caterpillars on curled parsley*

↓ *The trumpet-like blooms of honeysuckle*

→ *Water fountain with arch*

A Celebration of Seasons

A guide to entertaining and creating a warm and inviting atmosphere in the garden

Each season brings a new opportunity to revise the garden, plant anew, and decorate for that time of year. In addition to the interior of the farmhouse, I'm sure you've already surmised that I also enjoy decorating each aspect of my outdoor space including the greenhouse, farmhouse table, porch, and silo. I view it as an extension of the indoors, so why not use the space *you* have and expand your vision to include the outdoors? I love to bring creativity and joy when designing my outdoor spaces, and it is always my goal to create a low-maintenance, cozy, and relaxed feel.

I encourage you to find a source of inspiration when designing your outdoor décor for any event. Consider the colors you wish to include and the season or event you're celebrating. Inspiration can come from the simplest items: a photograph, a piece of art, the garden, or even a single color. In this chapter, we'll dive into some of the techniques I use to guide my design process through the changing seasons.

OUTSIDE-THE-BOX THINKING

Use creative ways to catch the eye when decorating. Think outside the box for unique and imaginative ways to make your space stand out.

And don't forget to think vertically! A creative use of display space is to hang items from above. The possibilities are endless. It's a great way to heighten interest in your current season and display unique and fun items in an unusual way.

DIY EFFORTS

At the beginning of my career in design, I was hesitant to include DIY projects. However, throughout the years, I've increasingly indulged in ideas that push my creative boundaries. As an example: the hanging roses in my greenhouse. We glued individual faux roses onto weighted fishing lines with hot glue and poured a significant amount of time and resources into this project. Be aware of the demanding nature of a project like this one. It took time but, for me, it was well worth the effort. The project turned out so beautifully, and it complements my greenhouse so well. I have not regretted taking this step for a second; I even duplicated this project in the fall, using fall leaves and witches' hats!

↑ *The interior of the greenhouse is adorned with hanging roses for spring.*

↑ *The greenhouse is ready for Halloween with floating witches' hats.*

A Space for Entertaining

My goal was to create a warm and welcoming space for outdoor dining, especially during pleasant weather. I set up a vintage farmhouse table just outside the greenhouse, beneath the old oak tree, which is an ideal spot for outdoor gatherings. I surrounded the table with an assortment of mismatched chairs collected during antique hunts. The mix of wooden and painted white chairs adds a relaxed, cottage-style allure to the space. I enjoy using a traditional farmhouse color palette in my designs, which helps make this area feel inviting, a perfect spot for friends and family to share a meal and enjoy the beauty of the garden.

↑ *The mercantile table in the greenhouse is all set for Christmas, featuring a tree in the corner where the plate rack usually sits.*

↑ *Christmas table setting by the greenhouse*

Entertaining is a big part of our time spent on the farm. We always entertain in the garden, especially when the temperatures are cool. Our antique silo is another perfect outdoor entertaining area. In fact, it is used primarily for entertaining and is decorated with metal gliders and chairs, which withstand the outdoor weather. I incorporate pillows and throw blankets to make it more cozy during the holidays. We installed a big screen television just under the entryway, and it has become our favorite place to watch fall football games and holiday movies!

Looking back on all our treasured times, my favorite holiday memory would have to be from last Christmas. The garden was flourishing with lots of greens and vegetables, and the silo was decorated to perfection with lights, trees, and even a hot cocoa bar I created from an old Ball canning jar advertisement stand. We enjoyed watching holiday movies while sipping on hot cocoa and eating marshmallows together.

While one of my favorite spaces on the farm is the silo, it is important to consider its location while decorating. I am frequently asked about the challenges presented with outdoor decorating, and how to navigate them. The weather in Texas is pleasant nearly year-round, so we are fortunate to be able to use all our outdoor areas most of the year. The only exception to this is the heat of the summer. During those months, I keep the décor lighter.

I constantly find myself repurposing vintage pots, tools, vases, risers, and baskets. While I do try to incorporate new pieces every year, the real magic is in rearranging old décor to keep things fresh. I always incorporate seasonal flowers and vegetables in my table arrangements. As the seasons progress, I simply replace the fresh elements of my décor, flowers, fruits, berries, etc., that are held in my repurposed items. Some examples of seasonal items include lemons and herbs in spring, tomatoes in summer, kumquats and pumpkins in fall, and various greens and cranberries.

If you are interested in using plants in your décor, but aren't sure where to start, I suggest planting what is in season in your area. This way, you can fill your space with seasonal décor and whatever produce is in season. Be sure to learn your hardiness zone and planting schedule for your climate (see chapter 1 for more information). Also, don't rely on big box stores to provide the correct plants for your area. I always recommend visiting specialty nurseries in your local region for the best plants. They will also have more knowledge about your specific zone, too. Once you plant, you can not only reap a bountiful harvest for your kitchen, but you can also use the plants and produce for decorating your seasonal tablescapes, too!

↑ *The silo decorated for Memorial Day*

The farm's most enchanting sight: our silo beautifully decorated for the holidays

↑ *Our spring Easter tablescape*

SPRING INSPIRATION

Spring is a magical season on the farm. The garden is freshly tilled, and the soil is enriched with top-quality organic matter to create the perfect environment for new growth. After prepping the beds, planting is such a fun and rewarding way to start the season. The garden is soon bursting with a mix of vegetables and flowers, and, of course, my beloved 'Peggy Martin' rose arch takes center stage with its most stunning display of the year!

It's also time to spruce up the silo and greenhouse, as spring cleaning is in full swing. The toolshed is reorganized, and any necessary paint touch-ups around the garden and silo are completed.

The farmhouse table is polished and ready for our first spring luncheon. With a mixture of new and vintage ceramic plates, I love to embrace a cheerful blue and yellow color scheme, perfectly bright and vibrant for the season!

SUMMER VIBES

Another enjoyable season is summer. Although it gets very warm down south, our vintage silo (circa 1890s) stays surprisingly cool all season long. As mentioned, we opted to open all sides of the silo to allow a southerly breeze to flow through. You can often find me there relaxing for lunch, after working in the garden either harvesting one of my favorite tomatoes ('Indigo Rose') or deadheading my vast zinnia collection. From Memorial Day through July Fourth, I display bunting lined across the greenhouse and along its sides. As the night cools, our family often enjoys movies in the silo. We also take time to enjoy candlelit dinners on the farmhouse table, just beneath the old oak tree. You'll often find a dispenser of lemonade on the table and fresh strawberries for dessert! I also love to incorporate décor for each season all around the silo, farmhouse table, and greenhouse. I believe in making things functional *and* aesthetically pleasing, so all three are decorated seasonally.

For Memorial Day and July Fourth celebrations, I collect assorted patterned dishes and linens, all with a red, white, and blue theme for decorating the farmhouse table. I incorporate various styles and sizes of flags and garlands to add extra touches throughout. For my garland, I use a thin rope base and tie different patterns of red, white, and blue ribbon in simple knots all along the desired length. I then hang one in the greenhouse and use one on a table centerpiece for added charm. One of my favorite new pieces is my slim Uncle Sam, which I place in the center of the silo, atop our vintage copper *cazo de cobre* pot table. I also add banner flags to the ceiling, which gently drape to our vintage chandelier. The cascading bulbs on a dimmer switch make for a dazzling display at night!

↑ *The farmhouse table and silo decorated for the Fourth of July*

A FANCIFUL FALL

My favorite season to decorate has always been fall. Since we live in south Texas, summer temperatures are quite toasty. The first fall cool front is always a welcome break. That is when my seasonal decorating sparks into action!

As temperatures drop, the silo becomes the perfect spot to take a quiet moment and savor the season after spending the day harvesting cool-season crops such as lettuce, broccoli, collard greens, cauliflower, mustard greens, and various herbs. In the evening, our family loves watching football games in the silo. The vintage metal gliders and chairs are adorned with comfy pillows, both new and antique, and vintage quilts for when the air turns chilly. Since the metal seating is designed for the outdoors, it stays out year-round.

↑ A closer look at the fall tablescape, featuring miniature pumpkins and fresh apples

VINTAGE TOOLS AS DÉCOR

One of my latest favorite finds is a trio of vintage garden tools from the Round Top Antiques Show. I mounted them directly to the wall of the house so they are easily seen from the garden and can remain there year-round. It's yet another way to add vintage charm to our countryside farmhouse. As with most of my vintage décor, I don't mind at all that they are left outside to weather; it only adds to the charm!

→ Vintage garden tools showcased on the farmhouse wall overlooking the garden

↑ Autumn harvest table setting with a side view of the greenhouse and pumpkin display shelves

We're fortunate to enjoy mild fall temperatures, making it perfect for fall candlelit dinners at the farmhouse table. I love a casual setup with an effortless approach. Mismatched chairs, dishes, and vintage cutlery only add to the charm of our farmhouse table. In the fall, you often find a dispenser of apple cider on the table and a crackling fire in the stone pit, ideal for making s'mores! Pumpkins are a must everywhere you look. I place them on the shelves around the greenhouse, along with fall-themed vintage signs. They also line the pathway to the silo and the porch steps. The porch's nine rockers and a bed swing are each adorned with cozy blankets and pillows. This is yet another beautiful spot on the farm to relax and enjoy the garden by day and the stars by night.

For Thanksgiving, we often enjoy an evening meal outdoors at the farmhouse table. I keep the table décor simple, incorporating new pieces each year but finding the real magic in rearranging old décor to keep things fresh. Seasonal flowers and vegetables are always part of my table arrangement for Thanksgiving. I love to use kumquats, pomegranates, bittersweet berries, and various fall greenery found around the farm.

↑ *A look at our cozy cocoa bar in the silo, stocked with all the seasonal essentials*

A WINTER WONDERLAND

Our hot cocoa bar is always a winter favorite, but thanks to our mild weather, we also have the most charming holiday dinner on our outdoor farmhouse table. I dress my tablescape for the season with traditional red and green décor, complemented by a bountiful harvest from the garden. I add fairy string lights intertwined in the centerpiece and candles on the table, in various sizes. Bistro lights wrapped around the garden, greenhouse, silo, and farmhouse table cast a warm, magical glow that perfectly captures the spirit of the season.

← *Our winter garden is brimming with cool-season vegetables, including several varieties of lettuce featured here. In the background, you'll spot our greenhouse, dressed for the season and topped with a charming vintage sign just above the door.*

Tips for Creating the Perfect Tablescape

Creating a tablescape is a fun way to celebrate any occasion. It's very easy; it just requires time and a little patience ... and some of your favorite vintage finds! Here is my process for creating any tablescape.

STEP 1:
CHOOSE A THEME.
Choose a theme, then build your tablescape around it.

STEP 2:
CHOOSE COLORS THAT COORDINATE WITH THE THEME.
Colors can be complementary (colors that are opposites on the color wheel) or monochromatic (various tones of one color).

↑ *Cobalt-blue-themed tablescape accented with touches of yellow and lemons for spring*

STEP 3:
GATHER YOUR DÉCOR.

Gather any appropriate décor you have on hand. My motto is always try using what you already have first!

I like to add many pieces into my table-scape. There is an easy rule to prevent the design from looking too chaotic. Be sure to group similar pieces for the most visual impact. This creates a more aesthetically pleasing look and leaves some empty space for the eye to "breathe." Examples of this technique include using color blocking or grouping pieces with matching materials (wood, metal, ceramic etc.). For example, use various greenery in similar pots made of the same material, in the same color.

STEP 4:
SET YOUR FOCAL POINT FIRST, THEN BUILD AROUND IT.

Striking focal points draw attention and spark inspiration. These can range from a simple floral arrangement to a piece of art or even a unique vintage find.

Invest in higher quality florals for tablescaping. Mix faux with fresh flowers to create a seamless look. Fresh greenery is always an inexpensive option to buy. By mixing the fresh with reusable faux, year after year, you create a cohesive look while saving money at the same time.

STEP 5:
ADD FRESH FRUIT.

Using seasonal fresh fruit in your table arrangements really elevates the look. For example, you could group fruit in small clusters along the length of the table, or you could use fruits in the base of a clear vase or glass bowl, add fresh flowers, and use it as a focal point.

It is essential to consider the scale of your tablescape. If you are in a more intimate setting, lower your focal point. For smaller scales, use this rule: Place your elbows on the table, then rest your chin on your hands. Look across the table; the height of your focal point should be no higher than your sight line. This ensures you can converse with individuals across the table from you. If outdoors (or at a much larger setting) taller arrangements are perfectly suitable.

STEP 6:
USE LAYERING AND INCORPORATE HERBS TO DISPLAY NAPKINS.

Don't be afraid to show off your layering and artistic skills here! Try layering plates, chargers, and napkins at each seat to create more interest. There are many ways to display napkins. For instance, you can simply fold a napkin and let it hang beneath a plate, shape it into a flower with a vintage brooch at the center for a bridal shower, or tie it with jute or twine string and tuck in sprigs of woody herbs like thyme or lavender for a spring garden party. For holiday napkin rings, consider using a simple plaid ribbon to tie cinnamon sticks and rosemary cuttings to the napkin. Or use a classic velvet ribbon with a small stem of winterberry or holly for winter. Napkin ring ideas are endless. Just use your imagination!

→ *Continued*

STEP 7:

MATCH YOUR DINNERWARE WITH THE THEME.

For plates and glasses, stick with your planned theme and color scheme.

Pro Tip

Don't have enough plates? No worries! Visit a local antique store for vintage plates of the same material, color, and theme. It creates a softer, more vintage feel while staying true to your theme. Mixing and matching can be just as beautiful, if not more.

STEP 8:

ADD DECORATIVE TREASURES.

Now it's time to add any decorative objects and touches that match your theme. Again, a mix of inexpensive items with a few treasures here and there helps elevate the look.

Pro Tip

Use risers under a few objects to create different heights and to add visual interest, rather than resting all items on the existing table surface. Creating visual variety with varying heights evokes a nice flow within your decor, as it encourages the eye to keep moving. I use risers in every space I decorate. Expanding your décor vertically gives the illusion that your space is larger.

STEP 9: HAVE FUN WITH IT!

This is the most important part. Showing off your tablescape at your event gives you an opportunity to demonstrate your decorating skills. Use this time to shine!

↑ *Our Christmas tablescape, featuring a breathtaking garland centerpiece made with bottle vases*

Dealing with Challenges

I am often asked, "How do you deal with challenges regarding outdoor decor?" The main challenge regarding outdoor décor is always the weather, specifically rain, and snow and freezing temperatures if you live in a cold climate. You are at the mercy of Mother Nature, so your décor must withstand the elements. That is why I choose to use metal furniture, signs, garden containers, etc. When we use the space, I soften covered areas with pillows, throw blankets, and seasonal décor. Once we are done using the outdoor area, I then bring the less weather-tolerant décor inside. Because our vintage wood table is outside year-round, I simply tarp it when it's not in use. It's okay if the vintage décor takes on minor weathering—this just adds to its farmhouse charm!

My best advice for decorating any space is to start by using what you already have and let it come together naturally. Look around your garden for natural elements to incorporate into your festive décor, and gather inspiration from magazines, influencers, and your favorite stores. Then, take that information and add your personal touch to make it your own! Many times, you probably already have what you need, and you can always reconfigure a space using the same items, year after year.

↑ *The fall greenhouse is decorated to warmly welcome guests into the garden.*

CREATE YOUR VISION GALLERY

Inspiration from my garden you can use for creating a warm and festive entertaining atmosphere, no matter the season or celebration.

↑ *Celebrating July 4th in the garden.*

↑ *Easter tablescape*

→ *A fall tablescape rich in autumn colors and accents*

↑ *The greenhouse adorned for the holidays*

↑ *Tiny ghosts make a home in the greenhouse for Halloween.*

→ *Throw pillows and blankets add cozy charm to the vintage bench.*

From Garden to Plate

My Favorite Seasonal Recipes Using Flavors from the Garden

Here are a few of my favorite recipes, based on seasonal flavors from the garden. Be it the first harvest of spring berries, the summer's spicy peppers, the root vegetables of autumn, or the green vegetables of winter, these recipes embody the flavor of each season. I hope they bring a touch of garden-fresh inspiration to your table as much as they have mine. I encourage you to enjoy the simple pleasures of these homegrown ingredients.

Linzer Cookies Filled with Homemade Raspberry Jam

INGREDIENTS

- 1¼ cups (138 g) sliced almonds
- ¾ cup (100 g) granulated sugar
- 2¼ cups (281 g) all-purpose flour
- 1 teaspoon lemon zest
- ½ teaspoon cinnamon
- ½ teaspoon kosher salt
- 1 cup (225 g) cold unsalted butter, cut into cubes
- 1 egg, plus 1 egg yolk
- 2 teaspoons vanilla
- 1 tablespoon (7.5 g) confectioners' sugar
- ¼ cup (80 g) raspberry jam

COOKIE CUTTERS

- One large, one small of the same shape

INSTRUCTIONS

1. In a food processor, combine the almonds, granulated sugar, flour, lemon zest, cinnamon, and salt. Pulse to combine.

2. Add the butter to the flour mixture and pulse until only small pieces of butter are visible.

3. Add the egg, egg yolk, and vanilla and process until a smooth dough forms.

4. Place the dough on a floured surface and divide in half. Shape and flatten into a disk 1-inch (2.5 cm) thick. Wrap each disk in plastic wrap and refrigerate for 1 hour.

5. Preheat the oven to 350°F (175°C). Prepare two 9 by 13-inch (23 by 33 cm) baking sheets with parchment paper.

6. On a floured surface, roll out one disk of dough until it is about ⅛ inch (3 mm) thick.

7. Use the larger cookie cutter to cut as many cookies as possible. Transfer to a prepared baking sheet.

8. Repeat with the second disk of dough, but this time, also use the smaller cookie cutter to cut a hole in the center of each cookie. Transfer to a prepared baking sheet.

9. Bake for 18 to 20 minutes, or until slightly golden. Transfer to wire racks and let cool for 5 minutes.

10. Use a sifter to dust cookies with confectioners' sugar. Spread ½ teaspoon of jam on each solid cookie. Top with a cutout cookie. Enjoy!

Summer

Easy and Authentic Jalapeño Salsa

INGREDIENTS

- 10 jalapeño peppers
- 2 tablespoons (30 ml) avocado oil
- Salt to taste

INSTRUCTIONS

1. Slice the tops off each jalapeño pepper and score lengthwise.

2. Add water to a medium stock pot and bring to a boil.

3. Place the peppers into the pot and boil for 25 minutes or until completely soft. Remove from pot, reserving 1 cup (235 ml) of the water, and let cool.

4. Place the cooled peppers in a blender. Add the 1 cup (235 ml) of jalapeño water, the avocado oil, and salt to taste.

5. Blend until your desired consistency and serve.

Fall

Old Fashioned Sweet Potato Pie

INGREDIENTS

- 2 medium sweet potatoes
- 2 eggs
- ½ cup (100 g) sugar
- 4 tablespoons (55 g) softened butter
- ¼ cup (60 ml) milk
- ¼ teaspoon cinnamon
- ¼ teaspoon nutmeg
- 1 teaspoon vanilla
- Pinch of salt
- Premade piecrust

INSTRUCTIONS

1. Preheat the oven to 400°F (200°C). Place the sweet potatoes on a baking sheet and bake for 1 hour, or until the potatoes can be pierced easily with a fork. Remove from the oven and let cool.

2. Once cool, remove the skin from the sweet potatoes and place into a blender or food processor, along with the rest of the ingredients (except the piecrust). Puree until smooth.

3. Place the piecrust onto a baking sheet and pour the puree into it.

4. Top with ¼ cup (50 g) sugar and allow to rest at room temperature for 15 minutes so the sugar can melt.

5. Bake at 300°F (145°C) for 1 hour, or until the sweet potato filling is set and starts to brown. Remove from the oven and serve warm.

Southern-Style Collard Greens

INSTRUCTIONS

1. In a medium stockpot over medium heat, heat the olive oil. Add the onions and cook until tender, about 5 minutes. Add the garlic and cook until fragrant, about 1 minute.

2. Add the chicken broth and cooked bacon, and let it come to a boil.

3. Reduce to a simmer. Stir in collard greens, salt, and pepper. Cook until the greens have reached desired tenderness, about 1 hour, stirring occasionally.

4. Serve with cornbread and enjoy!

INGREDIENTS

- 1 to 2 tablespoons (15 to 30 ml) olive oil (for the pan)
- 2 medium onions, chopped
- 4 garlic cloves, finely chopped
- 4 cups (946 ml) chicken broth
- Several cooked bacon slices
- 3 pounds (1.3 kg) collard greens
- Salt and pepper to taste
- Splash apple cider vinegar (optional)
- 2 tablespoons (26 g) sugar (optional)

↑ *View of the farmhouse and silo just across the pond*

Some Final Thoughts

To wrap things up, I hope you have enjoyed this look into the world of the vintage farmhouse garden style and our own farm here at Southern Home and Farm. Sharing my passion for gardening, design, and all things vintage is far more than a hobby; it is a way of life I truly enjoy sharing. Should you have questions, want advice, need a little inspiration, or simply love the art of design, vintage goods, gardening, and the outdoors, I am here and happy to connect. Please reach out and ask me any questions you may have; sharing the knowledge of gardening and design is my passion.

You can find me on Instagram **@SouthernHomeandFarm**, where I am often sharing updates, tips, and peeks into what I'm currently working on here on the farm. For more content and resources, visit my website at **www.SouthernHomeandFarm.com.** You can also subscribe to my newsletter there to get regular updates delivered right to your inbox. And don't miss out by signing up for my FREE Garden Planning and Design Guide while you're at it!

Thank you for joining me on this adventure, and I look forward to connecting with you as we continue celebrating all the joys of gardening, design, vintage wares, and the warmth of a well-loved home and outdoor space.

As always, Happy Gardening!

Resources

Amazon
@Amazon
www.amazon.com
Garden tools for people with disabilities

Ace Mart Restaurant Supply
@AceMartRestaurantSupply
www.acemart.com
Greenhouse wire racks

Antique Farm House
@AntiqueFarmhouse
www.AntiqueFarmhouse.com
Home furnishings and accessories

Botanic
@Shop.Botanic
www.ShopBotanic.com
Garden center and gifts
Topiaries

Cutting Edge Stencils
@CuttingEdgeStencils
www.cuttingedgestencils.com
Greenhouse floor stencils

Duluth Trading Company
@DuluthTradingCompany
www.DuluthTrading.com
Garden overalls and gloves

East Coast Trimming
@EastCoastTrimming
www.EastCoastTrimming.com
Vintage ribbons

Enchanted Gardens
@EnchantedGardensRichmond
www.MyEnchanted.com
Garden center and gifts

Gracie Wilkins
@GracieCustomInteriors
Vintage wares, design services,
and custom soft goods

Mary Knight
@OkRanchVintage
Farmhouse antiques, vintage seed cabinets and
seed boxes

Heather LaCoppola
@hen_picked
Artwork and vintage farmhouse finds
Hand-painted pillows

The Original Round Top Antiques Fair
@RoundTopAntiquesTexas
www.RoundTopTexasAntiques.com
Antique and vintage goods

Marsha Smith
@Cottonseed Trading Company
www.CottonseedTradingCompany.com
Farmhouse antiques
Vintage *cazo de cobre* pot

Acknowledgments

First and foremost, I want to express my gratitude to all the men in my family who provided the support, encouragement, and countless hours of hard work to help bring my dreams to life. None of this would be possible without them.

- To my father, for his unwavering love and support.
- To my uncle, always ready with a helping hand.
- To my father-in-law, who guided many of my projects with his meticulous eye for detail.
- To my husband, who inspired me to chase my dreams and supported me every step of the way.

And the women:

- To my daughter, who brings profound meaning to my life; her support throughout this book was immeasurable.
- To my friend Gracie: Thank you for uplifting me just when I needed it most.
- And to many others, including my wonderful followers on Instagram, who showed me kindness, friendship, and encouragement throughout my journey. I thank you.

About the Author

Rhonda Kaiser is a social media influencer focusing on all things garden, vintage home, and design. It is her passion to share her knowledge of both gardening and creative ways to make outdoor spaces more beautiful. She has been featured on many websites, Instagram accounts, and both national and regional magazines. She is also a recurring guest on *Houston Life*, which can be seen on Houston's NBC affiliate, where Rhonda enjoys returning to share segments on gardening, outdoor tablescapes, and design. She was also chosen as a *Better Homes & Gardens* Stylemaker for 2023 and 2024 (to date). To take a look at the beautiful outdoor space Rhonda has created at her own home, visit her on Instagram **@SouthernHomeandFarm** or on her website at **www.SouthernHomeandFarm.com**

Education: Texas A&M University, B.A. in Agricultural Economics

Also studied Interior Design at The Art Institute of Houston

Certification: Texas Master Gardener

Landscape design course at Texas A&M University

Print features in *Better Homes and Gardens, Woman's World, Texas Gardener, American Farmhouse Style, In Her Garden, Country Sampler Farmhouse Style, Garden Gate*, and *Flea Market Décor*

Web features: *Southern Living, House Digest, Gardening Know How,* Angi, Outdoor Guide, Hunker, and *Hobby Farms*

Index